W9-CAL-405

The Best of Mr. Food®

Slow-Cookin' Quickies

"With the ease and convenience of hands-off cooking, dinner's ready when you are! And 'OOH IT'S SO GOOD!!®'"

Roast with Red Wine Gravy, page 14, and
Oh-So-Simple Mashed Potatoes, page 15

Meaty Vegetable 'n' Rice Stuffed
Peppers, page 86

Blueberries 'n' Dumplings,
page 195

The Best of  Mr. Food®
Slow-Cookin' Quickies

Oxmoor House®

©2007 by Oxmoor House, Inc.
Book Division of Southern Progress Corporation
P.O. Box 2262, Birmingham, Alabama 35201-2262

All rights reserved. No part of this publication may be reproduced in any
form or by any means without the prior written permission of the publisher,
excepting brief quotes in connection with reviews written specifically for
inclusion in magazines or newspapers, or limited excerpts strictly for personal use.

ISBN-13: 978-0-8487-3151-9
ISBN-10: 0-8487-3151-4
Library of Congress Control Number: 2006908797

Printed in the United States of America
First Printing 2007

Mr. Food® and OOH IT'S SO GOOD!!® are registered marks owned by
Ginsburg Enterprises Incorporated.

Ginsburg Enterprises Incorporated
    Chief Executive Officer: Art Ginsburg
    Chief Operating Officer: Steven Ginsburg
    Vice President, Publishing: Caryl Ginsburg Fantel
    Vice President, Creative Business Development: Howard Rosenthal

Oxmoor House, Inc.
    Editor in Chief: Nancy Fitzpatrick Wyatt
    Executive Editor: Susan Carlisle Payne
    Managing Editor: Allison Long Lowery

THE BEST OF MR. FOOD® SLOW-COOKIN' QUICKIES, featuring the recipes of
Mr. Food, Art Ginsburg
    Editor: Kelly Hooper Troiano
    Nutrition Editor: Anne C. Cain, M.S., M.P.H., R.D.
    Senior Copy Editor: L. Amanda Owens
    Editorial Assistant: Rachel Quinlivan, R.D.
    Photography Director: Jim Bathie
    Senior Photo Stylist: Kay E. Clarke
    Associate Photo Stylist: Katherine Eckert
    Director, Test Kitchens: Elizabeth Tyler Austin
    Assistant Director, Test Kitchens: Julie Christopher
    Food Stylist: Kelley Self Wilton
    Test Kitchen Professionals: Kathleen Royal Phillips, Catherine Crowell Steele,
      Ashley T. Strickland
    Director of Production: Laura Lockhart
    Production Manager: Tamara Nall
    Production Assistant: Faye Porter Bonner

Contributors:
Designer: Carol Damsky
Indexer: Mary Ann Laurens
Editorial Assistant: Laura K. Womble
Interns: Jane Chambliss, Carol Corbin, Amy Edgerton,
    Amelia Heying, Caroline Markunas
Food Stylists: Ana Price Kelly, Debby Maugans
Test Kitchen Professionals: Mary Long, Kate Wheeler
Photographers: Beau Gustafson, Lee Harrelson
Photo Stylist: Lee Ann Montgomery

To order additional
publications, call
1-800-765-6400.

For more books to enrich
your life, visit
oxmoorhouse.com.

Cover: *Spicy Barbecue Beef Sandwiches, page 78*

Contents

Welcome!!

❝Slow cookers aren't just for pot roasts anymore! Sure, we've got that, too, but how 'bout decadent desserts?!? And savory sides?! Dust off that slow cooker, and turn the pages to discover:

- What's new in the slow-cooker market
- Tips for slow-cookin' ease
- 2 weeks' worth of slow cooker–inspired menus
- Simple one-dish meals that don't need all the extras
- Delicious dishes that require just 5 ingredients or less
- Lightened recipes for the health conscious

You'll be a slow-cooker genius with the help of:

- Easy-to-find ingredients and numbered step-by-step directions for every recipe
- Prep and cook times that take the guesswork out of meal planning
- Recipe tips and shortcuts to make slow cookin' fast

With the ease and convenience of 170 sensational new recipes, you'll agree when we say, 'Ooh it's slow good!'❞

Mr. Food

Slow-Cookin' Magic

> **"** Today's slow cookers are oh-so-easy to use—but, of course, I have a few tips for you that'll have you cooking up everything from appetizers to desserts! **"**

Sizin' Up Cookers

Today's slow cooker isn't like your mama's of yesteryear. This time-savin' appliance comes in oval and round shapes and in lots of sizes—from 1 quart up to 7 quarts and everything in between. You'll find up-to-date colors and lots of extras— such as an automatic on/off switch, programmable models with digital timers, crocks that can go from the freezer to the oven to the cooktop, and dual cookers that allow an entrée and side dish to cook at the same time.

All you have to do is choose the right size of slow cooker for your recipe. Most of our recipes give you two size options. For best results and food-safety issues when cooking entrées, use the size slow cooker that's called for in the recipe. If you use a different size than specified, know that cook times and consistency of the food may vary.

New on the market is an **external timer device** that allows you to set the cooking time. When the cooking time's up, the timer automatically switches the slow cooker to the WARM setting. Just plug the timer into the wall outlet, and then plug your cooker into the timer.

Marketplace Chatter

New cookers tend to cook faster than older models, so if you haven't bought a new slow cooker in the last year or two, I recommend you start shopping! Now's the best time to buy one because there's never been a better variety.

The appliances range from the cost-conscious but efficient standard units with HIGH and LOW switches to snazzier new models with all the bells and whistles. Here's a rundown of the fancier units.

The **Smart-Pot** comes in 5- and 6-quart sizes and is programmable to cook either 4 to 6 hours on HIGH setting or 8 to 10 hours on LOW setting. And it automatically switches to WARM when the cook time is complete!

For the fancy-schmancy set, check out the **Recipe Smart-Pot.** It has a database of over 250 recipes at the touch of a button, cook times that can be set at hour and half-hour increments, and a clear view of remaining cook time.

The **Smart-Set Programmable** slow cooker offers preset cook cycles for foods often slow-cooked, such as chicken, beef, and chili. Choose the setting, and the cooker tracks the food's temperature and knows when it's done.

A **VersaWare** cooker has a stoneware crock that can go straight from the freezer to the oven. It can even brown foods before cooking them.

Some cookers, such as the **Versatility Slow Cooker with Griddle,** now have a base that doubles as a griddle. So when the soup's done, you can fry up a grilled cheese to go alongside.

One especially portable model comes with a tote and plastic lid to slip on the crock after cooking so you can transport your slow-simmered specialty. The base of the cooker doubles as a warming dish for baking dishes.

Tips 'n' Techniques

Follow these important guidelines to ensure slow-cookin' success with your recipes.

• Remember that 1 hour on HIGH setting is equivalent to 2 hours on LOW setting. An advantage to cooking on LOW setting is that recipes can cook a little longer than the recipe states without the risk of the food being overdone.

• Always layer ingredients in the order given in the recipe. There's no need to stir the ingredients unless the recipe specifies.

• Trim excess fats from meats. You can also brown meat in a skillet or broiler to remove fat. Just be sure to drain the fat before adding the meat to the cooker.

• Pour liquids over meats, and use only the liquids specified in the recipe when cooking roasts and stews. Extra juices cook out of the ingredients, and less evaporation occurs than in traditional cooking methods.

• Cuts of meat that have a higher fat content can be cooked without additional liquid when set on LOW, though you may prefer to add a little liquid for making gravy.

• You can thicken juices and make gravy by removing the lid and cooking on HIGH setting for the last 20 to 30 minutes of cooking time.

• Don't be tempted to take a peek inside the cooker before cooking time is complete. It takes 20 to 30 minutes for the heat to build back up to the previous temperature after removing the lid.

Food Facts

• Slow cookers don't brown food, so sear **meats** or **poultry** in a skillet for extra flavor and added eye-appeal, as well as to cook off excess fat before adding to the cooker.

• Cut **whole chickens** and **large pieces of meat** in half before placing in the slow cooker to make sure they cook thoroughly.

• **Veggies** generally cook slower than meats. Place 'em under the meat in the slow cooker unless otherwise directed; direct contact is need-ed with the bottom and sides of the cooker.

• **Dairy** and **seafood** tend to break down when cooked for an extended time. Unless otherwise directed, add milk, cream, and sour cream during the last 15 minutes of cooking and put in seafood within the last hour.

• Fresh **herbs** and **spices** are better than the dried variety for extended slow-cookin' times because they take longer to release their flavors. When using dried herbs, opt for whole rather than crushed or ground.

• **Pasta** retains the best texture when cooked separately, according to package directions. Add cooked pasta to the slow cooker during the last 30 minutes of cooking unless other-wise directed.

• Long-grain converted **rice** is best in recipes that call for cooking rice in the slow cooker.

• Soak **dried beans** before adding them to the slow cooker, and add sugar and acid only after the beans have cooked until tender. Dried beans take longer to tenderize if com-bined with sugar and acid before softening.

11

Be Slow 'n' Safe

• Fill your slow cooker at least half full but no more than two-thirds full. This helps keep the temperature of the food even.

• Always cook raw meat and poultry dishes on HIGH setting for the first hour to speed up the time it takes to get to a safe temperature. Then you can reduce the heat to the LOW setting for the duration of the cooking time, if you'd like.

• You can forgo the HIGH setting for the first hour if the recipe calls for browning the meat first—precooking jump-starts the initial temperature of ingredients.

• Defrost any frozen foods before cooking a dish that includes meat, poultry, or seafood. This makes sure that the contents of the crock reach a safe temperature quickly.

Easy, Breezy Cleanup

• Let the slow-cooker insert cool completely before washing it. Running cold water over a hot insert may cause it to crack.

• Cleanup just got easier with new clear heavy-duty plastic liners that fit into 3- to 6½-quart oval and round slow cookers. Just insert a liner inside the slow cooker before adding your ingredients. When cooking is complete, serve your meal directly from the cooker.

Once the cooker has cooled (and the food is all gone or you've spooned it up for left-overs), simply toss the plastic liner—along with all the mess!

• If you're not using liners, be sure to coat the inside of the cooker with nonstick cooking spray for easier cleanup.

• Never immerse a slow cooker in water! Unplug it, and then wipe it clean with a cloth.

Test Kitchen Tidbits

• New slow cookers tend to cook at hotter temperatures than older models. If you're using a new model, check for doneness at the lower end of the time range. If your cooker tends to boil contents, check for doneness a little early.

• Some slow cookers have hot spots—where one side cooks hotter than the other. If you experience this with your cooker, rotate the insert halfway through the cooking time. This technique also allows for even browning of cobblers and crusts.

• Avoid soggy toppings, caused by condensation that collects on the slow-cooker lid dripping into the pot, by tilting the lid away from the food when removing it.

• Stews and casseroles cooked in the slow cooker tend to be forgiving in how long you cook them, so if you run a little late getting home, you're probably safe. Foods with dairy products and seafood are not good candidates for cooking longer than suggested.

Menu Marvels

··

66With this selection of slow cooker–inspired menus, you can put a meal on the table fast! I've paired traditional recipes to serve alongside and even have some dual slow-cooker options where two cook side by side, providing you a total no-fuss meal.99

Menu

Sunday Dinner
serves 6

Roast with Red Wine Gravy
Oh-So-Simple Mashed Potatoes
Steamed Broccoli

Roast with Red Wine Gravy

(pictured on page 2)

4 to 6 servings

prep: 10 minutes   cook: 8 hours and 1 minute

slow-cooker size: 5 quart

1   (2½-pound) boneless beef chuck
    shoulder roast, trimmed
¾   teaspoon pepper
1¾ cups dry red wine or low-sodium
    beef broth
1   (10¾-ounce) can cream of
    mushroom soup, undiluted
1   (1.2-ounce) package brown sauce
    mix

2   tablespoons cornstarch
2   tablespoons water

1 Sprinkle roast with pepper; place in a 5-quart slow cooker. Add wine, cream of mushroom soup, and brown sauce mix.

2 Cover and cook on HIGH setting 1 hour. Reduce heat to LOW setting, and cook 7 hours or until tender.

3 Transfer roast to a serving platter, reserving juices in slow cooker; keep warm. Whisk together cornstarch and water in a small bowl; slowly whisk into juices in slow cooker. Increase heat to HIGH setting, and cook, uncovered, 1 minute or until slightly thickened, whisking frequently. Serve roast with gravy.

Oh-So-Simple Mashed Potatoes

(pictured on page 2)

6 to 8 servings

prep: 3 minutes   cook: 3 hours

slow-cooker size: 3 or 3½ quart

1   (22-ounce) package frozen mashed
        potatoes
¼   cup butter
1   teaspoon salt
½   teaspoon pepper
2   cups half-and-half

Butter pats (optional)

1 Combine first 5 ingredients in a 3- or
    3½-quart slow cooker.

2 Cover and cook on LOW setting
    3 hours. Serve with butter pats,
if desired.

66*Don't sweat it if you don't have
another slow cooker handy to cook
up these mashed potatoes. Just use
your ol' standby version of pota-
toes or those tasty refrigerated ones from your
supermarket.*99

Menu

Cajun Night
serves 10 to 12

Mumbo Jumbo Cajun Gumbo
French Bread

Mumbo Jumbo Cajun Gumbo

10 to 12 servings

prep: 22 minutes   cook: 6 hours

slow-cooker size: 7 quart

½   cup all-purpose flour

2   pounds smoked sausage, cut into
    ¼" slices

1   (16-ounce) package frozen
    seasoning blend
2   teaspoons prepared minced garlic
6   cups chicken broth
1   (14½-ounce) can stewed Cajun
    tomatoes, undrained
2   bay leaves
1   tablespoon Worcestershire sauce
2   teaspoons Creole seasoning
2   teaspoons hot sauce
½   teaspoon dried thyme

1   rotisserie chicken, skinned, boned,
    and coarsely chopped
2   cups frozen cut okra
Warm cooked rice

1 Heat a large nonstick skillet over medium-high heat; add flour. Cook 12 minutes or until flour is toasted and light golden, stirring occasionally. Remove from pan; set aside.

2 Add sausage to pan. Cook sausage over medium-high heat 3 to 4 minutes or until browned. Drain, if needed.

3 Place sausage and flour in a 7-quart slow cooker; toss well to coat sausage. Stir in seasoning blend and next 8 ingredients.

4 Cover and cook on LOW setting 5 hours. Stir in chicken and okra; cover and cook on LOW setting 1 more hour. Serve over warm rice.

Menu

Busy Mom's Supper
serves 6

Rotisserie Chicken
Wild About Rice
Glazed Carrots

Wild About Rice

6 to 8 servings

prep: 5 minutes   cook: 3 hours or 6 hours

slow-cooker size: 4 quart

1   (6-ounce) package wild rice
¼   cup butter, cut into pieces
1   (8-ounce) package sliced fresh
        mushrooms
3   scallions, chopped
½   teaspoon salt
1   (14-ounce) can chicken broth
2   tablespoons sherry or water
½   cup sliced almonds, toasted

1 Combine first 7 ingredients in a 4-quart slow cooker.

2 Cover and cook on HIGH setting 3 hours or on LOW setting 5 to 6 hours or until rice is tender. Drain excess liquid, if necessary. Fluff rice with a fork; sprinkle with toasted almonds.

Glazed Carrots

Cut 1 pound of medium carrots diagonally into ¼"-thick slices. Cook carrots in boiling water to cover with ½ teaspoon salt for 5 minutes or until crisp-tender. Drain and rinse with cold water. Pat dry with paper towels.

Melt 2 tablespoons butter in a large skillet over low heat. Add ½ cup minced onion; cook, stirring constantly, 10 minutes. Add 1½ tablespoons brown sugar; cook, stirring constantly, 5 minutes. Add ⅔ cup apple juice; cook 10 minutes, stirring occasionally. Stir in carrots and ¼ teaspoon each of salt and pepper. Serves 6.

Menu
Down-home Favorites
serves 8

Homestyle Chicken 'n' Dressing
Pecan Green Beans

Homestyle Chicken 'n' Dressing

8 to 10 servings

prep: 29 minutes   cook: 4 hours or 7 hours

slow-cooker size: 5-quart round

1   large rotisserie chicken, skinned,
      boned, and shredded (about
      4 cups)
6   cups coarsely crumbled cornbread
      (see tip)
8   (1-ounce) slices firm white bread,
      torn into pieces
2   (14-ounce) cans chicken broth
2   (10¾-ounce) cans cream of chicken
      soup, undiluted
1   medium onion, chopped
3   celery ribs, chopped
4   large eggs, lightly beaten
2   teaspoons ground sage
½   teaspoon pepper
¼   teaspoon salt
½   cup butter, softened

1 Combine first 11 ingredients in a large
  bowl. Transfer mixture to a lightly
greased 5-quart round slow cooker. Dot
evenly with butter.

2 Cover and cook on HIGH setting 3 to
  4 hours or on LOW setting 7 hours
or until set. Stir well before serving.

❝Make the dressing even
easier by picking up already-
baked cornbread from the
deli at your local supermarket. Just steer
away from the sweet variety—savory is
definitely the way to go here.❞

Pecan Green Beans

8 servings

prep: 17 minutes   cook: 8 minutes

2   pounds small fresh green beans
½   teaspoon salt

½   cup chopped pecans
¼   cup butter, melted

1   teaspoon salt
¼   teaspoon pepper

1 Wash beans; trim stem ends. Cook beans and ½ teaspoon salt in a small amount of boiling water in a Dutch oven 4 to 5 minutes or until crisp-tender; drain beans, and return to pan.

2 Meanwhile, sauté pecans in butter in a medium skillet over medium-high heat until butter is lightly browned and pecans are toasted.

3 Pour butter-pecan mixture over beans; sprinkle with 1 teaspoon salt and the pepper, tossing gently to coat.

"Start these savory beans during the last 30 minutes of the chicken 'n' dressing cooking time. Then everything will be nice 'n' warm when you're ready to serve dinner."

Fall Gathering
serves 6

Slow-Simmerin' Beef Stew
Apple-Pecan Crisp

Slow-Simmerin' Beef Stew

6 to 8 servings

prep: 20 minutes   cook: 7½ hours

slow-cooker size: 5 to 6 quart

2   pounds round steak, cut into
      1" pieces
2   (1-pound) packages frozen stew
      vegetables
1   (8-ounce) package sliced fresh
      mushrooms
1   (14½-ounce) can diced tomatoes
      with green bell peppers and
      onions
1   (6-ounce) can tomato paste
¾   cup beef broth
⅓   cup red wine or beef broth
¼   cup all-purpose flour
2   cloves garlic, minced
1½ teaspoons salt
1   teaspoon pepper
½   teaspoon dried thyme

1 Combine all ingredients in a 5- to
6-quart slow cooker.

2 Cover and cook on LOW setting
7½ hours.

Apple-Pecan Crisp

6 servings

prep: 15 minutes   cook: 3 hours

slow-cooker size: 5 to 6 quart

5   large Granny Smith apples, peeled
      and cut into ¼"-thick slices
2   tablespoons lemon juice

¾   cup all-purpose flour
¾   cup packed dark brown sugar
1   teaspoon ground cinnamon
⅛   teaspoon salt
½   cup cold butter

¾   cup chopped toasted pecans
Vanilla ice cream

1 Place apples in a lightly greased 5- to 6-quart slow cooker; drizzle with lemon juice, and toss to coat.

2 Combine flour and next 3 ingredients in a medium bowl. Cut butter into flour mixture with a pastry blender or 2 forks until mixture resembles coarse meal; sprinkle over apples.

3 Cover and cook on HIGH setting 2 to 3 hours or until apples are tender. Sprinkle with pecans. Serve warm with ice cream.

Slow-Cooker Savvy

Be sure to check these apples at 2 hours—you don't want them to be mushy. If they need to continue to cook, remember to add 20 to 30 minutes to your cooking time, since the slow-cooker lid was removed.

Menu

Breakfast for the Kids
serves 3

"Apple Pie" Oatmeal
Crispy Brown Sugar Bacon
Orange Juice

"Apple Pie" Oatmeal

3 servings

prep: 8 minutes   cook: 8 hours

slow-cooker size: 3-quart oval

3   cups fat-free milk
1⅓ cups uncooked regular oats
½   teaspoon salt
¼   cup packed light brown sugar

3   tablespoons butter
¼   cup pure maple syrup

1   (12-ounce) package frozen harvest
        apples
Vanilla ice cream (optional)
Apple pie spice

1 Combine first 4 ingredients in a bowl, stirring well. Pour into a lightly greased 3-quart oval slow cooker.

2 Cover and cook on LOW setting 8 hours. Add butter, stirring until it melts. Stir in syrup.

3 Prepare apples according to package directions. Spoon oatmeal into bowls; top with ice cream, if desired, and apples. Sprinkle with apple pie spice, and serve immediately.

Crispy Brown Sugar Bacon

3 servings

prep: 15 minutes   cook: 25 minutes

½   pound hickory-smoked bacon slices
½   cup packed light brown sugar
1   to 1½ teaspoons cracked black
        pepper

1 Preheat the oven to 425°. Cut bacon slices in half. Combine sugar and pepper in a shallow dish. Dredge bacon in sugar mixture, shaking off excess.

2 Twist each bacon slice, if desired. Place bacon in a single layer on a lightly greased baking rack in an aluminum foil–lined baking pan.

3 Bake at 425° for 20 to 25 minutes or until crisp. Allow bacon to cool before serving.

66Every kids' dream—having ice cream for breakfast! Put this recipe on before you turn in for the evening, and I betcha everyone will be up bright and early for this treat! Add a little fancy-schmancy twist to the bacon—literally—by giving each slice a little twist before baking.99

Menu

Hearty Winter's Meal
serves 6

Pumpernickel Roast
Roasted Veggies

Pumpernickel Roast

6 servings

prep: 5 minutes   cook: 8 hours and 10 minutes

slow-cooker size: 4 quart

1   (10-ounce) package frozen pearl
      onions, thawed
1   (4-pound) sirloin tip roast
1   (12-ounce) bottle dark beer
¼   cup stone-ground mustard
1   tablespoon caraway seeds
1½ teaspoons salt
1   teaspoon pepper

⅓   cup all-purpose flour
Warm cooked medium-sized egg noodles

1 Place onions in a 4-quart slow cooker;
place roast on top. Add beer and next
4 ingredients.

2 Cover and cook on HIGH setting
8 hours or until roast is tender.
Remove roast and onions, reserving
drippings in cooker.

3 Briskly whisk flour into reserved drippings; cook on HIGH setting 10
more minutes or until thickened. Stir
gravy well, and serve gravy with roast,
onions, and warm noodles.

Roasted Veggies

6 servings

prep: 20 minutes   cook: 30 minutes

1½ pounds sweet potatoes, peeled and
    cut into 1½" pieces (2 medium)
¾ pound turnips, peeled and cut into
    1½" pieces (3 small)
1   large onion, peeled and cut into
    1½" wedges
6   cloves garlic, peeled
3   tablespoons olive oil

1   tablespoon chopped fresh or dried
    rosemary
1   tablespoon chopped fresh oregano
    or 1 teaspoon dried oregano
1   teaspoon salt

1 Preheat the oven to 450°. Combine first 5 ingredients in a large bowl; toss well. Arrange vegetables in a single layer in a large roasting pan or broiler pan.

2 Cook at 450° for 25 to 30 minutes or until well browned, stirring gently every 10 minutes.

3 Stir in herbs and salt just before serving.

"Sure, a lot of roast recipes put all the veggies in the slow cooker to cook everything at once, and they're good—just check out the ones on the following pages. But I like the idea of keeping these veggies separate from the meat and roasting them. It brings out their natural sweetness—and the high heat creates a crisp surface, sealing in all that good flavor."

Menu

Soup's On—Mexican Style!
serves 4

**Mexican Stew
Easy Cheesy Quesadillas**

Mexican Stew

4 servings

prep: 25 minutes   cook: 7 hours and 15 minutes

slow-cooker size: 5 quart

3   pounds stew beef
3   tablespoons canola oil, divided

6   tablespoons tomato paste
2   (10½-ounce) cans condensed beef
     broth, undiluted
1   teaspoon ground black pepper
6   cloves garlic, crushed
1   tablespoon chili powder
1½ teaspoons ground cumin
6   tablespoons chopped pickled
     jalapeños
1   cup water

2   tablespoons cornstarch
2   tablespoons cold water
Chopped fresh cilantro
Sour cream

1 Cut larger pieces of stew beef into bite-sized pieces. Heat 2 tablespoons oil in a large nonstick skillet over medium heat; add half the beef, and cook 8 minutes or until browned on all sides. Repeat with remaining oil and beef.

2 Place meat in a 5-quart slow cooker. Add tomato paste, beef broth, and next 6 ingredients. Stir well to blend.

3 Cover and cook on LOW setting 7 hours or until meat is very tender.

4 Combine cornstarch and water in a small bowl. Add to slow cooker; increase heat to HIGH setting, and cook, uncovered, 15 minutes or until thickened, stirring several times. Top stew with chopped cilantro, and serve with sour cream.

Easy Cheesy Quesadillas

4 servings

prep: 4 minutes   cook: 1½ minutes

¾ cup refried beans
4   (8") flour tortillas
1¼ cups (5 ounces) shredded Mexican
       cheese blend, divided
½   cup taco sauce, divided

Sour cream

1 Spread beans evenly over 2 tortillas. Sprinkle evenly with ¾ cup cheese, and drizzle with ¼ cup taco sauce. Top with remaining tortillas.

2 Microwave 1 quesadilla, covered with a paper towel, on a microwave-safe plate at HIGH 1 to 1½ minutes. Repeat procedure with remaining quesadilla. Cut each quesadilla into 4 wedges; serve with remaining taco sauce, remaining cheese, and the sour cream.

"I love the rich broth created when the stew cooks! And the jalapeños and chili powder give it just the right amount of oomph! It's good by itself or served over rice. And don't forget the quesadillas to round out this south-of-the-border menu!**"**

Menu

Slow, Southern Goodness
serves 8

Easy Brunswick Stew
Sour Cream Cornbread

Easy Brunswick Stew

8 servings

prep: 15 minutes   cook: 12 hours

slow-cooker size: 6 quart

3   pounds boneless pork shoulder roast
    (Boston butt)

3   medium-sized new potatoes, peeled
    and chopped
1   large onion, chopped
1   (28-ounce) can crushed tomatoes
1   (18-ounce) bottle barbecue sauce
1   (14-ounce) can chicken broth
1   (9-ounce) package frozen baby lima
    beans, thawed
1   (9-ounce) package frozen corn,
    thawed
6   tablespoons brown sugar
1   teaspoon salt

1 Trim excess fat from roast, and cut into 2" pieces.

2 Stir together roast, potatoes, and remaining ingredients in a 6-quart slow cooker.

3 Cover and cook on LOW setting 10 to 12 hours or until potatoes are fork-tender. Remove roast with a slotted spoon, and shred with 2 forks. Return shredded roast to slow cooker, and stir well. Ladle stew into bowls.

Sour Cream Cornbread

8 servings

prep: 10 minutes   cook: 20 minutes

1½ cups self-rising cornmeal mix
½   cup all-purpose flour
1   (15-ounce) can cream-style corn
1   (8-ounce) container fat-free sour
    cream
3   large eggs, lightly beaten
2   tablespoons chopped fresh cilantro
1   cup (4 ounces) shredded Cheddar
    cheese

1 Preheat the oven to 450°. Lightly grease a 10" cast-iron skillet. Heat skillet in the oven for 5 minutes.

2 Stir together cornmeal mix and flour in a large bowl; add corn and remaining ingredients, stirring just until blended. Pour batter into hot lightly greased skillet.

3 Bake at 450° for 18 to 20 minutes or until golden brown and cornbread pulls away from sides of skillet.

66You've got the Virginia version with lima beans, the Georgia version without lima beans, and now the Mr. Food slow-cookin' version with lima beans—but you can leave 'em out if you like! I'll let you decide which version of Brunswick Stew you like best. But, hands down, this hands-off version is definitely a winner in my book.99

Menu

Holiday Brunch
serves 8 to 10

Christmas Morning Strata
Fresh Fruit
Quick Mimosas or Orange Juice

Christmas Morning Strata

8 to 10 servings

prep: 10 minutes   cook: 3½ hours   chill: 8 hours

slow-cooker size: 5 quart

1	pound ground pork sausage
6	cups cubed French bread
2	cups (8 ounces) shredded smoked Gouda cheese
3	cups milk
6	large eggs, lightly beaten
2	teaspoons prepared mustard
¾	teaspoon Worcestershire sauce
¼	teaspoon salt
¼	teaspoon black pepper
¼	teaspoon ground nutmeg

1 Brown sausage in a large skillet over medium-high heat, stirring until it crumbles and is no longer pink; drain well.

2 Place bread cubes in a lightly greased 5-quart slow cooker; sprinkle sausage and cheese over bread.

3 Combine milk and remaining 6 ingredients in a medium bowl; pour over bread in slow cooker. Remove insert from slow cooker; cover insert, and chill 8 hours. Return insert to slow cooker, and let it stand at room temperature 20 minutes.

4 Cover and cook on LOW setting 3½ hours or until set.

Quick Mimosas
Pour equal parts chilled Champagne and orange juice into a pitcher, and—voilà—cocktails are served!

Menu

Summer Celebration
serves 4 to 6

Classic Barbecue Ribs
Coleslaw
Texas Toast

Classic Barbecue Ribs

4 to 6 servings

prep: 15 minutes   cook: 7 hours

slow-cooker size: 5 quart

4   pounds bone-in country-style pork
      ribs
2   teaspoons salt, divided

1   medium onion, chopped
1   cup packed light brown sugar
1   cup apple butter
1   cup ketchup
½   cup lemon juice
½   cup orange juice
1   tablespoon steak sauce
1   teaspoon coarse ground pepper
1   teaspoon minced garlic
½   teaspoon Worcestershire sauce

1 Cut ribs apart, if necessary, and trim excess fat; sprinkle 1 teaspoon salt evenly over ribs.

2 Stir together remaining 1 teaspoon salt, the onion, and remaining 9 ingredients until blended. Pour half of onion mixture into a 5-quart slow cooker. Place ribs in slow cooker, and pour remaining onion mixture over ribs.

3 Cover and cook on HIGH setting 6 to 7 hours or until ribs are tender.

❝Stop slavin' over the grill, and let your slow-cooker do all the cookin'! You'll be a barbecue genius because after one bite of these tender ribs, the gang will be oohing and aahing for more!❞

Menu

Island Delight
serves 4

Polynesian Shrimp
Chocolate-Coconut Bread Pudding (see page 200)

Polynesian Shrimp

4 servings

prep: 6 minutes   cook: 2½ hours

slow-cooker size: 3 quart

1   (20-ounce) can pineapple tidbits
      in juice
1   (6-ounce) package frozen snow
      peas, thawed
1   red bell pepper, cut into thin strips

2   tablespoons cornstarch
1   cup low-sodium fat-free chicken broth
1   tablespoon soy sauce
¼   cup packed brown sugar
½   teaspoon ground ginger
¼   teaspoon crushed red pepper

1   (16-ounce) bag frozen cooked
      medium shrimp, thawed
2   tablespoons cider vinegar
Warm cooked rice
1   teaspoon sesame seeds, toasted

1 Drain pineapple, reserving ½ cup juice. Place drained pineapple, snow peas, and red bell pepper in a 3-quart slow cooker.

2 Whisk together cornstarch, chicken broth, reserved pineapple juice, the soy sauce, and next 3 ingredients in a small saucepan. Bring mixture to a boil; cook, stirring constantly, 1 minute or until thickened. Add sauce to pineapple and vegetables in slow cooker.

3 Cover and cook on LOW setting 1½ to 2 hours. Stir in shrimp; cover and cook on LOW setting 30 more minutes or until heated through. Add vinegar, and stir gently. Serve over warm rice. Top each serving with toasted sesame seeds.

Simmering Starters

The only fussing required here is over your guests— not over the appetizers or beverages. These starters will keep 'til you're ready to serve 'em up!

Caponata

3¾ cups

prep: 18 minutes   cook: 3 hours or 6 hours

slow-cooker size: 3 quart

1	large eggplant, diced
½	teaspoon salt
1	tablespoon olive oil
1	large Rome apple, cut into ½" cubes
½	(12-ounce) jar roasted red bell peppers, drained and coarsely chopped
½	cup pitted kalamata olives, coarsely chopped
½	cup chopped red onion
1	clove garlic, pressed
¾	teaspoon dried oregano
¾	teaspoon ground cumin
¾	teaspoon capers
2	tablespoons chopped fresh parsley or 2 teaspoons dried parsley
2	tablespoons apple cider vinegar

1 Place eggplant in a medium-sized microwave-safe bowl, and toss with salt. Microwave at HIGH 8 minutes; gently toss with olive oil.

2 Stir together eggplant, apple, and next 8 ingredients in a 3-quart slow cooker. Cover and cook on HIGH setting 3 hours or on LOW setting 6 hours or until apples are tender. Stir in vinegar.

66 *Chock-full of vegetables and fruit, I like to serve this versatile Sicilian dish as a healthy dip or relish.* 99

Goat Cheese- and Herb Sausage-Stuffed Mushrooms

22 appetizers

prep: 30 minutes   cook: 2 hours

slow-cooker size: 6-quart oval

½   pound hot ground pork sausage
2   teaspoons prepared minced garlic

1   (4-ounce) package goat cheese
¼   teaspoon dried Italian seasoning

½   pound button mushrooms
    (about 22)

1 Cook sausage and garlic in a large skillet over medium-high heat, stirring until the sausage crumbles and is no longer pink. Drain sausage mixture, and return to skillet.

2 Reduce heat to medium; add cheese and Italian seasoning to sausage mixture, stirring until cheese melts. Remove from heat; cool slightly.

3 Clean mushrooms with damp paper towels. Remove stems, and reserve for another use.

4 Spoon sausage mixture evenly into mushroom caps. Place stuffed mushrooms in a single layer in a 6-quart oval slow cooker. Cover and cook on LOW setting 2 hours or until mushrooms are tender.

"You'll want to get out the big oval-shaped cooker for this recipe so these savory stuffed mushrooms will cook in a single layer. They're a cinch to put together for a party."

Sweet-Hot Wings

(pictured on facing page)

12 appetizer servings

prep: 27 minutes   cook: 4 hours   chill: 8 hours

slow-cooker size: 4 to 5 quart

5   pounds chicken wings (about 18)

1½ cups pure maple syrup
2   cups hot sauce (see note)
2   tablespoons Dijon mustard
2   teaspoons onion powder
1½ tablespoons Worcestershire sauce
1   teaspoon garlic salt

Blue cheese or Ranch dressing
Celery sticks

66These slow-cookin' wings are just the ticket when you're having the gang over—they stay nice and warm throughout the party. The gang will love the taste, and you'll love the convenience!99

1 Cut off and discard wing tips; cut wings in half at joint.

2 Combine syrup and next 5 ingredients in a small bowl, stirring well. Reserve 1½ cups marinade for serving as a dipping sauce; cover and chill. Pour remaining marinade into a large resealable plastic freezer bag; add chicken, and seal. Chill 8 hours, turning bag occasionally.

3 Preheat the broiler. Remove chicken from marinade, discarding marinade. Place chicken skin side up on a lightly greased rack in a broiler pan. Broil 3" from heat 10 to 12 minutes or until browned.

4 Place wings in a 4- to 5-quart slow cooker. Cover and cook on LOW setting 4 hours. Serve with reserved 1½ cups marinade, dressing, and celery sticks.

Note: For testing, we used a medium-heat hot sauce. If you choose to go with a hotter sauce, decrease the amount to 1½ cups.

French Dip Sandwich,
page 131

Slow-Cooker Lasagna,
page 88

Restaurant-Style Queso Blanco

(pictured on facing page)

6 cups

prep: 12 minutes   cook: 2 hours

slow-cooker size: 4 quart

1   small onion, diced

1½ teaspoons prepared minced garlic
1   (14½-ounce) can petite cut diced
        tomatoes with jalapeños, drained
1   (4.5-ounce) can chopped green
        chilies, undrained
1   cup milk
1½ teaspoons salt-free Mexican
        seasoning
½   teaspoon coarsely ground pepper
2   pounds white American cheese
        (from the deli)

Tortilla chips

1 Place onion in a medium-sized microwave-safe bowl; cover loosely with heavy-duty plastic wrap. Microwave at HIGH 2 minutes.

2 Combine onion, garlic, and next 5 ingredients in a 4-quart slow cooker. Tear cheese slices into large pieces. Add cheese to slow cooker, stirring until blended.

3 Cover and cook on LOW setting 2 hours (do not overcook). Stir cheese dip before serving; keep warm. Serve with tortilla chips.

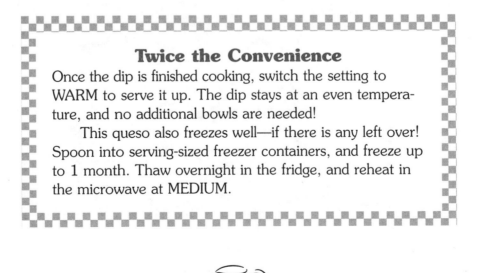

Twice the Convenience

Once the dip is finished cooking, switch the setting to WARM to serve it up. The dip stays at an even temperature, and no additional bowls are needed!

This queso also freezes well—if there is any left over! Spoon into serving-sized freezer containers, and freeze up to 1 month. Thaw overnight in the fridge, and reheat in the microwave at MEDIUM.

Spicy Beer 'n' Cheddar Fondue

3 cups

prep: 12 minutes   cook: 1 hour

slow-cooker size: 3-quart oval

½   cup milk

1   (8-ounce) block sharp Cheddar
      cheese, shredded

1   (8-ounce) block Monterey Jack
      cheese with peppers, shredded

2   tablespoons cornstarch

½   teaspoon salt

½   teaspoon garlic powder

¼   teaspoon ground red pepper

¾   cup beer (see tip)

Cubed French bread and/or sliced pears

1 Heat milk in a medium saucepan over medium heat 1 to 2 minutes or just until it begins to simmer, stirring occasionally.

2 Meanwhile, toss together cheeses and next 4 ingredients in a small bowl.

3 Add cheese mixture a handful at a time to hot milk, stirring until fondue is smooth and beginning to bubble.

4 Pour fondue into a 3-quart oval slow cooker; stir in beer. Cover and cook on LOW setting 1 hour. Serve with cubed bread and/or sliced pears.

Note: Serve fondue within 2 hours. (See tip on page 43.)

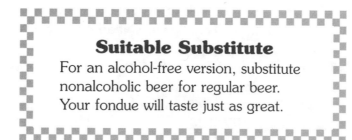

Suitable Substitute

For an alcohol-free version, substitute nonalcoholic beer for regular beer. Your fondue will taste just as great.

Smoky Chili Con Queso

4½ cups

prep: 8 minutes   cook: 2 hours

slow-cooker size: 3 quart

1   pound hot ground pork sausage

2   cups shredded smoked Cheddar
      cheese
1   (16-ounce) jar pasteurized prepared
      cheese product, cubed
1   (16-ounce) jar fire-roasted salsa
½   cup milk
½   teaspoon chipotle chili powder

Tortilla chips

1 Cook sausage in a large skillet over medium-high heat, stirring until it crumbles and is no longer pink; drain.

2 Stir together sausage, cheeses, and next 3 ingredients in a 3-quart slow cooker. Cover and cook on LOW setting 2 hours or until cheese melts. Serve with tortilla chips.

66 *Cheese dips aren't as forgiving as other dishes prepared in a slow cooker, when an extra hour or so of cooking wouldn't make a difference in the end results. Do not cook longer than 2 hours and be sure to serve within 2 hours to prevent separation caused by the dip getting too hot.* 99

Buffalo Chicken Ranch Dip

6½ cups

prep: 10 minutes   cook: 3 hours

slow-cooker size: 3 to 4 quart

3   cups shredded cooked chicken
      (see tip)
1   cup hot sauce
2   (8-ounce) packages cream cheese,
      softened
1   (8-ounce) container sour cream
1   (1-ounce) package Ranch dressing
      mix

Celery sticks
Assorted corn chips, tortilla chips, or
      crackers

1 Combine first 5 ingredients in a 3- to 4-quart slow cooker. Cover and cook on LOW setting 3 hours.

2 Stir dip before serving. Serve with celery sticks, corn chips, tortilla chips, or crackers.

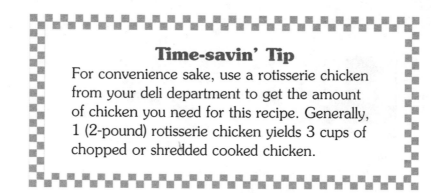

Time-savin' Tip
For convenience sake, use a rotisserie chicken from your deli department to get the amount of chicken you need for this recipe. Generally, 1 (2-pound) rotisserie chicken yields 3 cups of chopped or shredded cooked chicken.

Hot Parmesan-Artichoke Dip

6 cups

prep: 18 minutes   cook: 3½ hours

slow-cooker size: 3 quart

1½ cups mayonnaise
2   (12-ounce) jars marinated quartered
      artichokes, drained and chopped
½   teaspoon hot sauce
2   cups freshly grated Parmesan
      cheese
4   cloves garlic, minced

Toasted baguette slices or assorted
      crackers

1 Stir together first 5 ingredients.
Spoon into a 3-quart slow cooker.

2 Cover and cook on LOW setting
3½ hours or until light golden. Stir
well before serving. Serve with baguette
slices or assorted crackers.

*66This favorite dip is as tasty as ever and
can be served straight from the slow
cooker—a sure crowd-pleaser!99*

Warm Honey and Fruit Spread

2½ cups

prep: 7 minutes   cook: 2½ hours

slow-cooker size: 3 quart

2	(8-ounce) packages cream cheese, cubed and softened
½	cup honey
½	cup chopped dried fruit
¼	cup chopped pecans
2	teaspoons orange marmalade
¼	teaspoon ground cinnamon

1 Beat cream cheese and honey at medium speed of an electric beater until creamy. Stir in dried fruit and remaining ingredients.

2 Spoon into a 3-quart slow cooker. Cover and cook on LOW setting 2½ hours. Stir before serving.

Sweet Options
This versatile spread pairs well with biscuits or scones as a chunky topper. Or spread it over shortbread cookies for a simple dessert.

Spiced Caramel Apple Cider

7 cups

prep: 3 minutes   cook: 4 hours

slow-cooker size: 3½ quart

1   (64-ounce) container apple cider
⅓   cup caramel topping
1½ teaspoons apple pie spice, divided

Fresh whipped cream
Additional caramel topping

1 Stir together cider, ⅓ cup caramel topping, and 1 teaspoon apple pie spice in a 3½-quart slow cooker. Cover and cook on LOW setting 4 hours.

2 Pour cider through a fine wire-mesh strainer; discard spice. Ladle into individual mugs, and dollop with whipped cream. Sprinkle with remaining ½ teaspoon apple pie spice, and drizzle with additional caramel topping.

"If you like caramel apples, try this cider that's simmered with caramel sauce and apple pie spice. It's just what the doctor ordered on a chilly autumn day. Don't forget to dollop each serving with whipped cream and extra caramel sauce!"

Warm Honey Russian Tea

6¾ cups

prep: 5 minutes   cook: 2 hours or 4 hours

slow-cooker size: 3 quart

3   (3") cinnamon sticks
10   whole cloves

6   cups water
⅓   cup orange-flavored breakfast
       beverage crystals
⅓   cup presweetened lemonade mix
¼   cup unsweetened instant tea
¼   cup honey

1 Tie cinnamon sticks and cloves in a cheesecloth bag.

2 Stir together water and remaining 4 ingredients in a 3-quart slow cooker; add spice bag. Cover and cook on HIGH setting 2 hours or on LOW setting 4 hours. Remove and discard spice bag; stir well before serving.

Tea Service
Reduce your slow-cooker setting to LOW or WARM when serving to keep the tea warm throughout your gathering. Any leftovers will easily heat up in a small saucepan on your cooktop—or try it over ice.

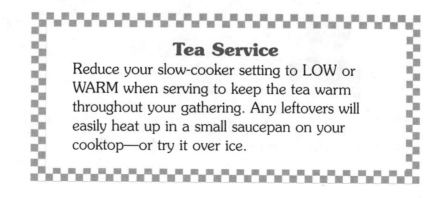

Warm Winter-Spiced Punch

5 cups

prep: 4 minutes   cook: 4 hours

slow-cooker size: 3 to 4 quart

2   cups pomegranate juice
1½ cups cranberry juice cocktail
1   cup apple juice
⅓   cup orange juice
¾   cup sugar
4   whole cloves
2   (3") cinnamon sticks
1   lemon, cut into ¼"-thick slices
1   thin-skinned orange, cut into
       ¼"-thick slices

1 Combine first 7 ingredients in a 3- to 4-quart slow cooker; stir until sugar dissolves. Float lemon and orange slices on top. Cover and cook on LOW setting 4 hours. Remove cloves and cinnamon sticks before serving.

Thin Skinned?

Be sure to use a thin-skinned orange, such as Valencia or Hamlin, to avoid bitterness. The thicker skin of a navel orange will impart a bitter flavor during the long cooking time.

Mulled White Wine Punch

6½ cups

prep: 5 minutes   cook: 2½ hours

slow-cooker size: 3 quart

2   (3") cinnamon sticks
6   whole cloves
6   whole allspice
2   cups white cranberry juice
½   cup water
½   cup orange juice
2   tablespoons honey
⅓   cup sugar
1   tablespoon lemon juice
1   (750-milliliter) bottle Pinot Grigio

1 Combine all ingredients in a 3-quart slow cooker (see tip).

2 Cover and cook on LOW setting 2½ hours. Remove and discard cloves and cinnamon sticks before serving.

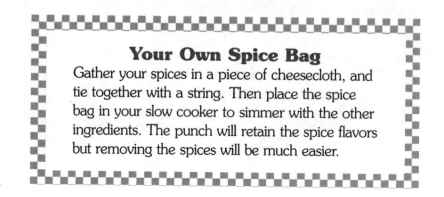

Your Own Spice Bag

Gather your spices in a piece of cheesecloth, and tie together with a string. Then place the spice bag in your slow cooker to simmer with the other ingredients. The punch will retain the spice flavors but removing the spices will be much easier.

Super Soups & Stews

66Soups and stews are ideal for long simmers in the slow cooker! And most of these recipes are forgiving if you go over the cook time. So bring your appetite, and warm your soul with these wonderful bowls of comfort.99

Creamy Bell Pepper 'n' Tomato Soup

11 servings

prep: 7 minutes   cook: 5 hours

slow-cooker size: 4 to 5 quart

2   (28-ounce) cans crushed tomatoes
1   (14-ounce) can seasoned chicken
      broth with roasted garlic
4   whole bottled roasted red bell
      peppers, drained
2   tablespoons butter
1   (1.37-ounce) package thick and
      zesty spaghetti sauce mix
1   tablespoon sugar

2   cups half-and-half
¼   teaspoon ground red pepper
Freshly grated Parmesan cheese

1 Process first 4 ingredients, in batches, in a blender until smooth. Pour into a 4- to 5-quart slow cooker. Whisk in sauce mix and sugar.

2 Cover and cook on LOW setting 5 hours or until thoroughly heated.

3 Stir in half-and-half and ground red pepper. Sprinkle with Parmesan cheese.

66This isn't your mom's tomato soup! I've jazzed it up with roasted red bell peppers and cream. Yum-my! Don't try to save on calories and use milk or fat-free half-and-half. These products tend to curdle in the slow cooker, and the soup's pretty perfect as is.99

French Onion Soup

4 servings

prep: 10 minutes   cook: 4 hours and 15 minutes

slow-cooker size: 3 or 3½ quart

2	slices bacon
2	tablespoons butter, melted
2	medium-sized sweet onions, sliced
¼	teaspoon salt
⅛	teaspoon pepper
2	(10½-ounce) cans beef consommé
¼	cup dry white wine or water
1	cup restaurant-style croutons
4	slices Swiss cheese

1 Cook bacon in a skillet until crisp; remove bacon, reserving 1 tablespoon drippings in skillet. Reserve bacon for another use.

2 Combine drippings, melted butter, and next 3 ingredients in a 3- or 3½-quart slow cooker. Stir well to coat onions.

3 Cover and cook on HIGH setting 4 hours. Stir in consommé and wine; cover and cook on HIGH setting 15 more minutes or just until heated. Ladle soup into bowls; top each serving with ¼ cup croutons and 1 slice cheese.

❝For this recipe, an oval-shaped slow cooker helps to caramelize the onions more evenly because there's more surface area for the onions to cook. However, the resulting soup is fantastic made in a round slow cooker, too. You can also cook the soup on LOW setting for 8 hours, but the onions won't caramelize as much.**❞**

Pesto Vegetable Soup

8 to 10 servings

prep: 17 minutes   cook: 6½ hours

slow-cooker size: 5 to 6 quart

2   (14-ounce) cans seasoned chicken
     broth with roasted garlic
1   cup chopped onion
1   (10-ounce) package frozen petite
     peas
1   (9-ounce) package frozen cut green
     beans
1   large zucchini, chopped
2   (14½-ounce) cans petite-cut
     tomatoes, drained
2   (15-ounce) cans cannellini beans,
     drained and rinsed
1   teaspoon pepper

2   tablespoons pesto sauce
1   (6-ounce) bag fresh baby spinach,
     washed
Grated Parmesan cheese
Additional pesto sauce

1 Combine first 8 ingredients in a 5- to
6-quart slow cooker.

2 Cover and cook on LOW setting
6 hours; stir in 2 tablespoons pesto
sauce and the spinach. Cover and cook
on LOW setting 30 more minutes. Serve
with grated Parmesan cheese and additional pesto sauce.

*You'll be sure to pack in
your daily veggie count
with a bowl of my Pesto
Vegetable Soup. Soup's on—so eat up!*

Loaded "Baked" Potato Soup

8 servings

prep: 5 minutes   cook: 4 hours or 8 hours

slow-cooker size: 4 to 5 quart

2   (20-ounce) packages refrigerated
       diced potatoes with onion
1   (32-ounce) container chicken broth
¼   cup butter
2   teaspoons garlic salt
1¼ teaspoons freshly ground black
       pepper
1   (10¾-ounce) can cream of potato
       soup, undiluted

1   (8-ounce) container sour cream
1½ cups (6 ounces) shredded extra-
       sharp Cheddar cheese, divided
3   tablespoons chopped fresh chives
4   fully cooked slices bacon, chopped

1 Combine first 6 ingredients in a
  4- to 5-quart slow cooker.

2 Cover and cook on HIGH setting
  4 hours or on LOW setting 8 hours
or until potatoes are tender.

3 Mash mixture until potatoes are
  coarsely chopped and soup is slightly
thickened; stir in sour cream, 1 cup
cheese, and the chives. Ladle into individual bowls, and sprinkle each serving
with bacon and remaining cheese.

66 This rich soup has all the fixin's of a
loaded baked potato and is just as tasty. I
use refrigerated potatoes that are already
diced with onions. How's that for easy? 99

Creamy Chicken and Mushroom Soup

8 to 10 servings

prep: 20 minutes   cook: 3½ hours or 7 hours

slow-cooker size: 5 to 6 quart

3   celery ribs, thinly sliced (about
        1½ cups)
1   cup chopped onion
1   (8-ounce) package sliced fresh baby
        Portobello mushrooms
1   rotisserie chicken, skin and bones
        removed, and shredded into bite-
        sized pieces (see tip)
1   (10¾-ounce) can cream of
        mushroom soup, undiluted
1   (10¾-ounce) can cream of chicken
        soup, undiluted
4   cups water

1 Stir together all ingredients in a 5- to 6-quart slow cooker.

2 Cover and cook on HIGH setting 2½ to 3½ hours or on LOW setting 6 to 7 hours.

Time-savin' Chicken

Jump-start this recipe by picking up a rotisserie chicken at the deli counter of your supermarket. Generally, a 2-pound rotisserie chicken yields about 3 cups of chopped or shredded cooked chicken. Also check out the prechopped vegetables that are readily available in most produce departments these days. Talk about convenience!

Cheesy Mac 'n' Chicken Soup

7 servings

prep: 8 minutes   cook: 6 hours

slow-cooker size: 5 to 6 quart

1   small onion, diced
1   celery rib, diced
2   (14-ounce) cans low-sodium fat-free
    chicken broth
1   (16-ounce) package frozen mixed
    vegetables
1   (10¾-ounce) can cream of chicken
    soup, undiluted
2   cups chopped cooked chicken

1   (16-ounce) package pasteurized
    prepared cheese product, cubed
1   (20-ounce) package frozen macaroni
    and cheese

1 Combine first 6 ingredients in a 5- to 6-quart slow cooker.

2 Cover and cook on LOW setting 4 hours. Remove cover; add cheese and frozen macaroni and cheese. Cover and cook on LOW setting 2 more hours or until cheese melts and soup is thoroughly heated.

66 *Time-savin' convenience products, like the frozen mac 'n' cheese and mixed veggies, are a big help in putting together this slow-cookin' favorite.* 99

Southwestern Chicken Tortilla Soup

4 servings

prep: 5 minutes   cook: 6 hours

slow-cooker size: 3½ or 4 quart

2   cups chopped cooked chicken
2   (14-ounce) cans chicken broth
1   (14½-ounce) can diced tomatoes
     with garlic and onion, undrained
1   (11-ounce) can yellow corn with red
     and green bell peppers
1   (10¾-ounce) can tomato purée
2   teaspoons fajita seasoning
1   teaspoon chili powder

1   cup crushed tortilla chips
Chopped fresh cilantro

1 Combine first 7 ingredients in a
  3½- or 4-quart slow cooker.

2 Cover and cook on HIGH setting
  6 hours. Top each serving evenly
with crushed tortilla chips and cilantro
before serving.

66 *Swing by the supermarket, and pick
up a rotisserie chicken to use in this
soup. It not only adds great flavor, but
also saves you a lot of time when getting dinner on
the table. Generally, you'll get 3 cups of chopped
chicken from a rotisserie chicken.*99

Pasta e Fagioli Soup

8 to 10 servings

prep: 22 minutes   cook: 6 hours

slow-cooker size: 5 to 6 quart

1   pound ground chuck
1   cup chopped onion

3   cups chicken broth
2   (14½-ounce) cans diced tomatoes
        with basil, garlic, and oregano,
        undrained
1   (15-ounce) can tomato sauce with
        roasted garlic
1   (10-ounce) package frozen chopped
        spinach, thawed and well drained
1   (15-ounce) can kidney beans, rinsed
        and drained
½   teaspoon salt
½   teaspoon crushed red pepper

1   cup small seashell pasta, uncooked
Shredded Parmesan cheese

1 Cook beef and onion in a large skillet over medium-high heat about 5 minutes, stirring until the beef crumbles and is no longer pink; drain.

2 Place beef mixture in a 5- to 6-quart slow cooker; stir in broth and next 6 ingredients.

3 Cover and cook on LOW setting 5½ hours. Add pasta, and cook on LOW setting 30 more minutes or until pasta is tender. Ladle into individual bowls, and sprinkle each serving evenly with Parmesan cheese.

Italian Lesson

Fagioli is the Italian word for "beans," referring to the kidney beans that are used in this recipe. For a bit more flare, in place of Parmesan, shred some Asiago cheese over the soup. You'll enjoy its rich, nutty flavor.

Two-Bean Taco Soup

10 servings

prep: 12 minutes   cook: 5 hours

slow-cooker size: 6 to 7 quart

1½ pounds ground chuck

1   (1¼-ounce) package taco
     seasoning mix
1   (1-ounce) package Ranch dressing
     mix
2   (15¼-ounce) cans whole kernel
     corn with red and green bell
     peppers, undrained
1   (16-ounce) can pinto beans,
     undrained
1   (15-ounce) can black beans,
     undrained
1   (28-ounce) can diced tomatoes with
     garlic and onion
1   (4.5-ounce) can chopped green
     chilies, undrained
1   (14-ounce) can beef broth

Toppings: shredded Cheddar cheese,
     sour cream, tortilla chips, chopped
     fresh cilantro

1 Cook beef in a large skillet over
  medium-high heat, stirring until it
crumbles and is no longer pink; drain.

2 Combine meat, taco seasoning mix,
  and next 7 ingredients in a 6- to
7-quart slow cooker.

3 Cover and cook on LOW setting
  5 hours. Serve with desired toppings.

66 *This is a sure crowd-pleaser—
it makes 15 cups! Just pop the
tops of these canned goods, and
dump 'em all in your slow cooker with the
ground beef. Then forget about it—at least for
the next 5 hours!* 99

Meaty Tomato-Vegetable Soup

9 servings

prep: 12 minutes   cook: 9 hours

slow-cooker size: 5 to 6 quart

1   pound ground round
1   cup frozen chopped onion
1   tablespoon prepared minced garlic

2   (28-ounce) cans fire-roasted diced
      tomatoes
1   (10½-ounce) can condensed beef
      broth, undiluted
1½ cups water
1   (14½-ounce) can diced tomatoes
      with Burgundy wine and olive oil,
      undrained
1   (14½-ounce) can diced tomatoes
      with basil, garlic, and oregano,
      undrained
1   (16-ounce) package frozen mixed
      vegetables, thawed
½   teaspoon crushed red pepper

1 Cook beef, onion, and garlic in a large skillet over medium-high heat 7 minutes, stirring until the beef crumbles and is no longer pink; drain well.

2 Combine beef mixture, diced tomatoes, and remaining 6 ingredients in a 5- to 6-quart slow cooker.

3 Cover and cook on LOW setting 9 hours.

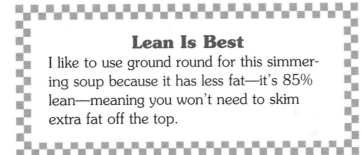

Lean Is Best

I like to use ground round for this simmering soup because it has less fat—it's 85% lean—meaning you won't need to skim extra fat off the top.

Steak 'n' Tater Soup

9 servings

prep: 14 minutes   cook: 9 hours

slow-cooker size: 5½ to 7 quart

2   tablespoons vegetable oil
1½ pounds round steak, cut into
       ½" cubes

1   cup all-purpose flour
6   cups water, divided
1   (14½-ounce) can stewed tomatoes,
       undrained
1   (16-ounce) package frozen mixed
       vegetables
3   cups peeled, chopped baking
       potatoes
1   cup diced carrots
1   cup diced celery
¼   cup beef-flavored bouillon granules
1   (1-ounce) package onion soup mix
1   teaspoon sugar
¼   teaspoon salt
¼   teaspoon pepper

1 Heat oil in a large nonstick skillet over medium-high heat. Add steak, and cook 10 minutes or until browned. Place in a 5½- to 7-quart slow cooker.

2 Combine flour and 3 cups water, stirring until smooth. Pour over steak in slow cooker. Add remaining 3 cups water, the tomatoes, and remaining ingredients to slow cooker.

3 Cover and cook on LOW setting 9 hours.

" *This hearty soup will satisfy even the biggest appetites. It's loaded with potatoes, veggies, and, of course, steak. Eat up, and enjoy!* **"**

New Year's Soup

6 servings

prep: 11 minutes   cook: 10 hours   soak: 8 hours

slow-cooker size: 6 quart

1   (16-ounce) package dried black-eyed
     peas

3   (14-ounce) cans seasoned chicken
     broth with roasted garlic
2   (14½-ounce) cans diced tomatoes
     with celery, onion, and green bell
     pepper
1   (10-ounce) can diced tomatoes and
     green chilies
1   (10-ounce) package frozen chopped
     onion
2   cups diced cooked ham
¾   teaspoon salt
¾   teaspoon freshly ground black
     pepper
1   (1-pound) package chopped fresh
     collard greens

Hot sauce

1 Place peas in a 6-quart slow cooker. Cover with water 2" above peas; let soak 8 hours (see note). Rinse and drain; return peas to slow cooker.

2 Stir broth and next 6 ingredients into peas; add greens.

3 Cover and cook on HIGH setting 10 hours or until peas and greens are tender. Serve with hot sauce.

Note: Before you turn in for the night, soak the peas and they'll be ready for the slow cooker the next morning.

Filled to the Brim
Adding the whole package of collard greens to the slow cooker will fill it up to the brim, but don't worry about it over-flowing. Just place the cover over the slow cooker, and allow a few hours for the greens to wilt.

Chunky Split Pea Soup

8 servings

prep: 17 minutes   cook: 8 hours   soak: 8 hours

slow-cooker size: 5 to 6 quart

1   (16-ounce) package dried split peas
5   large carrots, chopped (about
        2 cups)
1   cup chopped onion
3   celery ribs, chopped (about 1 cup)
1½ cups diced cooked ham
¼   teaspoon ground red pepper
¼   teaspoon ground cloves
4   cups water
1   tablespoon ham base (see tip)
½   teaspoon salt
½   teaspoon freshly ground black
        pepper
2   (14-ounce) cans seasoned chicken
        broth with roasted garlic
1   bay leaf

1¼ cups four cheese- and garlic-flavored
        croutons

1 Place peas in a 5- to 6-quart slow
  cooker. Cover with water 2" above
peas; let soak 8 hours (see note). Drain
and rinse; return peas to slow cooker.
Add carrots and next 11 ingredients to
slow cooker.

2 Cover and cook on LOW setting
  8 hours or until peas are tender and
soup is thick. **Remove and discard
bay leaf.** Ladle into individual bowls;
top evenly with croutons.

Note: Soak the peas the night before,
and they'll be ready for the slow cooker
the next morning.

Ham Base
Look for ham base in the supermarket
near the bouillon. It's liquid, as opposed to
the dried varieties.

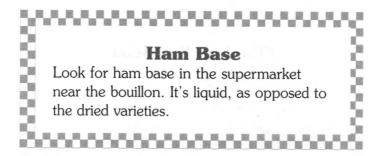

Spicy Sausage Soup

about 7 servings

prep: 20 minutes   cook: 6 hours

slow-cooker size: 5 to 6 quart

1   pound hot pork sausage

1   (1-pound) bag chopped fresh kale
        greens
1   medium onion, chopped
1   (16-ounce) can kidney beans
1   (32-ounce) container beef broth
1   (28-ounce) can crushed fire-roasted
        tomatoes
1   teaspoon ground cumin
1   teaspoon salt
½   teaspoon pepper

1 Cook pork in a large nonstick skillet over medium-high heat 7 minutes, stirring until it crumbles and is no longer pink.

2 Place kale in a 5- to 6-quart slow cooker; add pork, onion, and remaining ingredients.

3 Cover and cook on HIGH setting 6 hours or until kale is tender.

Not Just for Decoration
The attractive, frilly leaves of kale aren't just for garnishes anymore. With its mild, cabbagelike flavor, you're likely to see it more in salads, in stews, and as a side dish—as well as in soups, like this one.

Southwestern Corn Chowder

6 servings

prep: 25 minutes   cook: 4 hours or 8 hours

slow-cooker size: 4 to 5 quart

1   (20-ounce) package refrigerated
      diced potatoes with onion
1   (16-ounce) package frozen whole
      kernel corn
1   (10-ounce) package frozen
      seasoning blend
2   (14-ounce) cans seasoned chicken
      broth with roasted garlic
12 slices bacon, cooked and crumbled
1½ tablespoons chili powder
½   teaspoon salt

1   cup whipping cream
Toppings: shredded Cheddar cheese,
      coarsely crushed corn chips

1 Combine first 7 ingredients in a
4- to 5- quart slow cooker.

2 Cover and cook on HIGH setting
4 hours or on LOW setting 8 hours.

3 Stir in cream. Using a potato
masher, partially mash potatoes in
slow cooker until chowder is desired consistency. Serve with desired toppings.

Turn It Up!
If heat is what you're after,
mince a whole jalapeño pepper
and toss it in the chowder
mixture before cooking.

Big-Batch Kickin' Chili

10 servings

prep: 18 minutes   cook: 6 hours or 10 hours

slow-cooker size: 6 to 7 quart

4   pounds ground chuck
2   cloves garlic, minced

2   (14½-ounce) cans diced tomatoes
       with green bell pepper and onion,
       undrained
1   (10-ounce) can chili-style diced
       tomatoes with green chilies,
       undrained
2   (15-ounce) cans tomato sauce for
       chili
1   tablespoon sugar
1   (1.25-ounce) package chili
       seasoning
½   teaspoon ground red pepper
2   (16-ounce) cans light red kidney
       beans, rinsed and drained

Toppings: sour cream, shredded sharp
       Cheddar cheese, sliced scallions,
       sliced ripe olives

1 Cook beef and garlic, in batches, in a large skillet over medium-high heat 5 minutes, stirring until the beef crumbles and is no longer pink; drain.

2 Place mixture in a 6- to 7-quart slow cooker; stir in tomatoes and next 6 ingredients.

3 Cover and cook on HIGH setting 5 to 6 hours or on LOW setting 10 hours. Serve chili with desired toppings.

Freeze It!
If this is too much of a good thing for you, this chili freezes great. Divide leftover chili equally into 1-gallon resealable plastic freezer bags; seal and lay each bag flat. Freeze up to 1 month.

Chorizo and Black Bean Chili

(pictured on page 106)

6 servings

prep: 15 minutes   cook: 5 hours

slow-cooker size: 3½ or 4 quart

2   (12-ounce) packages fresh chorizo
      sausage, casings removed

2   (15-ounce) cans black beans, rinsed,
      drained, and divided
1   cup frozen chopped onion
1   cup chopped celery
1   cup grated carrot
1   (14-ounce) can reduced-fat
      less-sodium chicken broth
1   tablespoon dried oregano
3   tablespoons lemon juice
½   teaspoon pepper
1½ teaspoons prepared minced garlic

Sour cream

1 Cook sausage in a large skillet over medium-high heat, stirring until it crumbles and is no longer pink; drain.

2 Mash 1 can black beans with a fork in a small bowl. Combine sausage, mashed beans, remaining can of black beans, the onion, and next 7 ingredients in a 3½- or 4-quart slow cooker.

3 Cover and cook on LOW setting 4 to 5 hours. Serve with sour cream.

66 *Mashing 1 can of the black beans will help thicken the chili— making it ooh so good!* 99

Texas Turkey Chili

6 servings

prep: 11 minutes   cook: 3 hours or 6 hours

slow-cooker size: 3½ or 4 quart

1¼ pounds lean ground turkey
1   large onion, chopped
1   large green bell pepper, chopped
2   cloves garlic, minced
1   (28-ounce) can crushed tomatoes
1   (15-ounce) can black beans, drained
1   (11-ounce) can whole kernel corn,
        rinsed and drained
1   (8-ounce) can tomato sauce
1   (1.25-ounce) package chili
        seasoning mix
½   teaspoon salt

Toppings: shredded Colby and Monterey
        Jack cheese blend, tortilla chips

1 Cook first 4 ingredients in a large skillet over medium-high heat, stirring until the turkey crumbles and is no longer pink; drain. Spoon mixture into a 3½- or 4-quart slow cooker. Stir in tomatoes and next 5 ingredients.

2 Cover and cook on HIGH setting 3 hours or on LOW setting 6 hours. Serve with desired toppings.

Your Choice
Choose the cooking time that best fits your busy schedule—generally 1 hour on HIGH setting equals 2 hours on LOW setting.

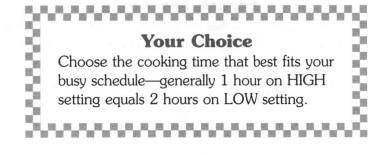

Quick Provençal Daube

6 to 8 servings

prep: 10 minutes   cook: 8½ hours

slow-cooker size: 4 to 5 quart

2 pounds chuck roast, trimmed and
    cut into 1" pieces
1 pound carrots, cut into 1" pieces
4 small yellow onions, cut into wedges
12 cloves garlic, peeled and halved
    lengthwise
1 (14½-ounce) can diced tomatoes
2 cups beef broth
2 tablespoons tomato paste
1 (1-ounce) envelope herb gravy mix
    for beef
1 teaspoon freshly ground pepper

1 Combine all ingredients in a 4- to 5-quart slow cooker.

2 Cover and cook on HIGH setting 1 hour. Reduce heat to LOW setting, and cook 7½ hours.

French Lesson

Daube is a hearty beef stew that is made in the south of France during the winter months. Traditionally, daube is slow-cooked and then refrigerated to mellow the flavors, but this version is quick to the table. If you want to follow tradition, prepare the recipe and cook as directed; let cool, and then set the ceramic insert of the slow cooker in the refrigerator to chill overnight. When ready to reheat, let insert stand at room temperature, and then cover and cook on HIGH setting 1 hour; reduce to LOW setting, and cook 1 hour. Serve it with a crusty baguette.

Camp Stew

12 servings

prep: 15 minutes   cook: 8 hours

slow-cooker size: 6 to 7 quart

1   pound ground beef
1   medium onion, chopped

2   large potatoes, peeled and diced
1   (16-ounce) package frozen speckled
       butter beans or lima beans,
       thawed
1   (14¾-ounce) can creamed corn
1   (8¾-ounce) can whole kernel corn,
       drained
1   (10-ounce) can barbecued pork
1   (10-ounce) can white chicken in
       water, drained
2   (14½-ounce) cans stewed tomatoes
1   cup ketchup
1   cup water
2   to 4 tablespoons lemon juice
1   tablespoon Worcestershire sauce
1   teaspoon hot sauce
1   teaspoon salt
1   teaspoon pepper

1 Cook ground beef and onion in a large skillet over medium-high heat stirring until the beef crumbles and is no longer pink; drain.

2 Layer potatoes, butter beans, beef mixture, creamed corn, and remaining ingredients in a 6- to 7-quart slow cooker.

3 Cover and cook on LOW setting 8 hours or until potatoes are tender.

"Chock-full of meat and vegetables, this is the ideal cold-weather dish for your family.**"**

Hoppin' John Stew

10 servings

prep: 6 minutes   cook: 6 hours

slow-cooker size: 5 to 6 quart

4   (15.8-ounce) cans black-eyed peas,
    undrained
2   (14½-ounce) cans diced tomatoes
    with celery, onion, and green bell
    pepper, undrained
1   (4.5-ounce) can chopped green
    chilies
1   (10½-ounce) can condensed beef
    broth, undiluted
1   cup water
1   pound smoked sausage, sliced
½   teaspoon garlic powder
¼   teaspoon pepper
1   cup uncooked long-grain rice

1 Combine all ingredients in a 5- or 6-quart slow cooker.

2 Cover and cook on LOW setting 6 hours.

Lots of Luck

Hoppin' John is typically a dish of black-eyed peas that's cooked with salt pork and seasonings and served with rice. It's a Southern tradition to serve this dish on New Year's Day to bring good luck in the coming year. But don't wait till then—give it a try any day of the year.

Hunter's Stew

5 servings

prep: 10 minutes   cook: 7 hours

slow-cooker size: 3½ or 4 quart

2	pounds smoked Polish sausage, diagonally sliced into 1" pieces (see tip)
1	large cooking apple, peeled, cored, and sliced
1	(30-ounce) package fresh sauerkraut, 2 tablespoons juice reserved
1	medium onion, chopped
1	(14½-ounce) can diced tomatoes, undrained
3	slices bacon, cooked and crumbled

1 Place all ingredients, including 2 tablespoons reserved sauerkraut juice, in a 3½- or 4-quart slow cooker, layering in order listed.

2 Cover and cook on LOW setting 7 hours.

66 *This stew got its name because it was the food of choice taken by Polish hunters on hunting trips. For more authentic taste, substitute Polish sausage for the smoked sausage. Pair this stew with rye or pumpernickel bread and a full-bodied beer for a one-dish meal that's sure to please the heartiest eater.* 99

Beefy Vegetable Stew

10 servings

prep: 17 minutes   cook: 7 hours

slow-cooker size: 4 to 5 quart

2	pounds beef round roast, cut into 1" cubes
2	teaspoons salt
1	teaspoon pepper
¼	cup all-purpose flour
1	tablespoon vegetable oil
1¼	cups beef broth
2	baking potatoes, diced
4	carrots, sliced
1	medium onion, chopped
1	celery rib, chopped
1	clove garlic, minced
1	teaspoon paprika
1	bay leaf
½	cup dry red wine or beef broth
1	teaspoon Worcestershire sauce

1 Sprinkle beef evenly with salt and pepper; toss with flour to coat. Heat oil in a large skillet over medium-high heat. Add beef, and cook 5 minutes or until browned on all sides; place beef in a 4- to 5-quart slow cooker.

2 Add beef broth to skillet, and scrape the bits from the bottom, using a wooden spoon; pour mixture over beef in slow cooker.

3 Add potatoes and remaining ingredients; stir well.

4 Cover and cook on LOW setting 7 hours or until meat and vegetables are tender. **Remove and discard bay leaf.**

Savvy Subs

You can substitute lamb for the beef in this hearty stew, or even try a venison round roast. Serve bowlfuls with French bread or sourdough bread and your favorite red wine to suit.

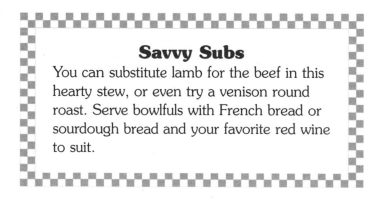

Beef Brisket with Citrus Sweet Potato Medley

8 to 10 servings

prep: 18 minutes   cook: 5 hours

slow-cooker size: 7 quart

1   tablespoon vegetable oil
2   (2-pound) beef briskets, trimmed
2   medium onions, sliced
1   orange, thinly sliced
1   pound carrots, peeled and cut into
        ½"-thick slices
1   pound sweet potatoes, peeled and
        cut crosswise into ½"-thick slices
1   medium Granny Smith apple,
        peeled and cut into 1"-thick slices

1   cup orange juice
2   tablespoons brown sugar
2   tablespoons ketchup
2   teaspoons dried thyme
½   teaspoon ground cloves
1   (14-ounce) can low-sodium fat-free
        chicken broth
¾   cup dry white wine or low-sodium
        fat-free chicken broth
2   (3") sticks cinnamon, broken in half
1   cup dried cranberries

1 Heat oil in a large nonstick skillet over medium-high heat. Add beef; cook 4 minutes on each side or until browned. Place onions in a 7-quart slow cooker; top with beef and orange slices. Add carrots, potatoes, and apple.

2 Whisk together orange juice and remaining 8 ingredients in a medium bowl. Pour mixture over beef.

3 Cover and cook on HIGH setting 4 to 5 hours or until meat and vegetables are tender. Transfer beef to a serving platter. Pour remaining vegetable mixture through a wire-mesh strainer, reserving juices and vegetables; discard cinnamon sticks. Serve beef and vegetable medley with juices.

66Try serving this brisket and vegetable medley over cooked noodles drenched with the warm citrus juices. It makes for an ooh-so-yummy meal!99

Slow & Easy Entrées

....

66With minimal prep time in the morning, dinner simmers through the day, thanks to your slow cooker. Then you can greet your family with a home-cooked meal and the 3 words everybody loves to hear, 'Dinner is served!'99

Beef Burgundy

6 servings

prep: 22 minutes   cook: 8 hours

slow-cooker size: 4 to 5 quart

3   tablespoons butter
1   (3-pound) rump roast or beef
        round, cut into 1½" cubes

1   large onion, sliced
1   clove garlic, minced
¼   cup all-purpose flour
1   cup dry red wine
1   (10½-ounce) can condensed beef
        broth, undiluted
2   tablespoons tomato paste

1   teaspoon dried thyme, crushed
1   bay leaf
½   pound frozen pearl onions
1   (8-ounce) package small fresh
        mushrooms
1   teaspoon salt
¼   teaspoon pepper

Warm cooked egg noodles

1 Melt butter in a large skillet over medium heat. Add beef, and cook 8 to 10 minutes or until thoroughly browned on all sides. Transfer beef to a 4- to 5-quart slow cooker, reserving drippings in skillet.

2 Add onion and garlic to drippings in skillet; sauté over medium heat 5 minutes or until tender, stirring frequently. Stir in flour; cook, stirring constantly, 1 minute. Slowly stir in wine, broth, and tomato paste; cook 1 to 2 minutes or until sauce coats the back of a wooden spoon.

3 Add thyme and next 5 ingredients to sauce; pour mixture over beef in slow cooker.

4 Cover and cook on LOW setting 8 hours. **Remove and discard bay leaf.** Serve over noodles.

66 *For the fancy-schmancy crowd, this dish is also known as Beef or Boeuf Bourguignon. Ooh la la!* **99**

Spicy Barbecue Beef Sandwiches

(pictured on cover)

10 servings

prep: 10 minutes   cook: 9 hours

slow-cooker size: 4 quart

1   (3½-pound) chuck roast
2   teaspoons garlic salt, divided

1   (10½-ounce) can condensed beef
      broth, undiluted
1   cup ketchup
½   cup packed light brown sugar
⅓   cup cider vinegar
1   teaspoon chili powder
1   teaspoon Worcestershire sauce
½   teaspoon ground red pepper

10   sandwich buns
Dill pickle slices (optional)

1 Cut roast in half; sprinkle with 1 teaspoon garlic salt.

2 Stir together remaining 1 teaspoon garlic salt, the beef broth, and next 6 ingredients in a medium bowl. Place roast into a 4-quart slow cooker; pour broth mixture over roast.

3 Cover and cook on HIGH setting 9 hours. Remove roast from slow cooker; shred meat with 2 forks. Serve meat on sandwich buns with sauce from slow cooker and, if desired, dill pickles.

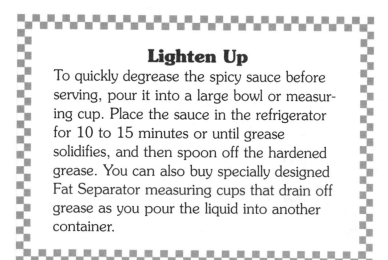

Lighten Up

To quickly degrease the spicy sauce before serving, pour it into a large bowl or measuring cup. Place the sauce in the refrigerator for 10 to 15 minutes or until grease solidifies, and then spoon off the hardened grease. You can also buy specially designed Fat Separator measuring cups that drain off grease as you pour the liquid into another container.

Fajita Beef 'n' Rice

6 to 8 servings

prep: 7 minutes   cook: 9 hours

slow-cooker size: 5- to 6-quart round

1   (4-pound) boneless top chuck roast
2   teaspoons fajita seasoning
2   (14½-ounce) cans Mexican-style
       stewed tomatoes, undrained

6   cups warm cooked rice
⅓   cup chopped fresh cilantro or fresh
       parsley
¼   cup lime juice

1 Trim excess fat from roast. Rub both sides of roast evenly with fajita seasoning. Place roast in a 5- to 6-quart round slow cooker; top with stewed tomatoes.

2 Cover and cook on HIGH setting 9 hours or until meat shreds easily with a fork. Remove roast from slow cooker, and shred using 2 forks. Degrease tomato liquid, discarding fat. (See tip on opposite page.) Stir shredded beef into tomato liquid.

3 Combine rice, cilantro, and lime juice. Serve beef mixture over rice.

ROH-pah VYAY-hoh

This recipe is similar to the Cuban dish *ropa viejo,* literally meaning "old clothes." Don't be scared off by that name 'cause this dish is traditionally made with leftover meat—usually pot roast—that's shredded and cooked in a spicy tomato sauce. It's scrumptious!

Saucy Italian Pot Roast

10 servings

prep: 10 minutes   cook: 6½ hours

slow-cooker size: 6 quart

1   (8-ounce) package sliced fresh baby
     Portobello mushrooms
1   large onion, cut in half and sliced
1   (2½- to 3-pound) boneless chuck
     roast, trimmed
1   (1.6-ounce) package garlic-and-herb
     sauce mix
½   teaspoon crushed red pepper
2   (14½-ounce) cans Italian-style diced
     tomatoes, undrained
1   (8-ounce) can no-salt-added tomato
     sauce

2   tablespoons cornstarch
2   tablespoons water

1 Place mushrooms and onion in a 6-quart slow cooker; add roast. Sprinkle roast evenly with sauce mix and crushed red pepper. Pour diced tomatoes and tomato sauce over roast.

2 Cover and cook on HIGH setting 5 to 6 hours or until meat is very tender. Remove roast from slow cooker, and cut into large chunks; keep warm.

3 Skim fat from juices in slow cooker; discard fat. Stir together cornstarch and water in a small bowl until smooth; add to juices in slow cooker, stirring until blended.

4 Cover and cook on HIGH setting 20 to 30 more minutes or until mixture is thickened, stirring once. Add roast pieces back to slow cooker. Cover and cook until thoroughly heated.

Winning Sides
Try this saucy pot roast over egg noodles, rice, or—for more authentic Italian flavor—polenta. It's a winner whichever way you choose!

Slow 'n' Easy Sauerbraten

6 servings

prep: 13 minutes   cook: 8 hours and 15 minutes   marinate: 8 hours

slow-cooker size: 5-quart oval

1	(3- to 4-pound) rump roast
1	cup water
1	cup white vinegar
1	medium onion, sliced
1	lemon, sliced
10	whole cloves
6	peppercorns
3	bay leaves
2	tablespoons salt
2	tablespoons sugar
1	tablespoon olive oil
15	gingersnaps, finely crushed

1 Place roast in a large resealable plastic freezer bag. Combine water and next 8 ingredients; pour over meat. Seal and marinate in the refrigerator 8 hours, turning meat occasionally.

2 Remove meat from marinade, reserving 1½ cups marinade; discard remaining marinade and bay leaves. Pat meat dry with paper towels. Heat oil in a large skillet over medium-high heat. Add beef; cook 3 to 4 minutes on each side or until thoroughly browned. Transfer beef to a 5-quart oval slow cooker; pour reserved marinade over meat.

3 Cover and cook on LOW setting 7 to 8 hours or until tender. Transfer roast to a serving platter, reserving juices in slow cooker; keep roast warm.

4 Add crushed gingersnaps to juices in slow cooker. Increase to HIGH setting; cover and cook 12 to 15 minutes or until gingersnaps are dissolved and gravy is thickened. Stir well. Serve roast with gravy.

Sprechen Sie Deutsche?

Serve this tender marinated beef and sauce over spaetzle—tiny noodles or dumplings—for a classic German dish.

Marinated Flank Steak

5 servings

prep: 2 minutes   cook: 4 hours   marinate: 8 hours

slow-cooker size: 5 quart

2   (1½- to 2-pound) flank steaks, each
      cut into 3 or 4 pieces
1   (8-ounce) bottle Italian salad
      dressing

¼   cup dried minced onion
2   tablespoons fajita seasoning
1   (14-ounce) jar roasted red bell
      peppers, drained and sliced
1   (4.5-ounce) can chopped green
      chilies

1 Place steak and dressing in a large
  resealable plastic freezer bag.
Marinate in the refrigerator 8 hours or
overnight.

2 Drain all but ⅓ cup dressing from
  steak. Place steak and reserved dressing in a 5-quart slow cooker; top with
onion and remaining ingredients.

3 Cover and cook on HIGH setting
  4 hours. Remove meat, and shred
with 2 forks. Place meat back into slow
cooker before serving. Serve steak using
a slotted spoon (see tip).

66You'll want to place your shredded meat
back into the slow cooker before serving so
the meat can absorb all of these flavorful
juices that remain. Warmed cooked polenta or mashed
potatoes make a nice bed in which to nestle the juicy
shredded meat. **99**

Feisty Fajitas

4 to 6 servings

prep: 5 minutes   cook: 4 hours or 7 hours

slow-cooker size: 4 quart

1½ pounds flank steak, cut into
        4 pieces
1   (10-ounce) package frozen
        seasoning blend, thawed
2   cloves garlic, pressed
1   (4.5-ounce) can chopped green
        chilies
1   (1.12-ounce) package fajita
        seasoning
1   (10-ounce) can diced tomatoes with
        lime juice and cilantro, drained
        (see tip)

Flour tortillas
Toppings: shredded Cheddar cheese,
        sour cream, salsa

1 Place steak in a 4-quart slow cooker; top with seasoning blend and next 4 ingredients.

2 Cover and cook on HIGH setting 4 hours or on LOW setting 7 hours. Remove meat, and shred with 2 forks; return meat to slow cooker. Spoon mixture onto tortillas using a slotted spoon; serve with desired toppings.

❝The next time you're at the supermarket, check out all the varieties of canned tomatoes on the shelves. You're sure to find one for almost every taste! If you can't find what's called for here, just use regular diced tomatoes in a similar size and stir in some chopped fresh cilantro and fresh lime juice.❞

Pepper Steak

6 servings

prep: 13 minutes   cook: 7 hours and 12 minutes

slow-cooker size: 4 quart

2 pounds top round steak (1" thick), trimmed
2 tablespoons vegetable oil
1 (14½-ounce) can peeled tomato wedges, undrained
2 large green bell peppers, cut into 1" strips

1 small onion, chopped
1 clove garlic, minced
¼ cup soy sauce
1 teaspoon sugar
1 teaspoon salt
¼ teaspoon black pepper
¼ teaspoon ground ginger

1 tablespoon cornstarch
½ cup cold water
Warm cooked noodles or rice

1 Cut steak into 3" pieces. Heat oil in a large skillet over medium-high heat. Add steak to skillet, and cook until browned. Transfer steak to a 4-quart slow cooker. Add tomatoes and bell pepper strips.

2 Combine onion and next 6 ingredients in a small bowl; pour over mixture in slow cooker.

3 Cover and cook on HIGH setting 7 hours. Combine cornstarch and water in a small bowl, stirring until smooth. Stir into mixture in slow cooker; cook, uncovered, on HIGH setting 12 minutes or until mixture is thickened, stirring often. Serve over noodles or rice.

❝You're guaranteed a tender piece of meat with every bite of this hearty dish. It cooks for 7 hours in your slow cooker—on HIGH! The gang will definitely think that you've been home cookin' all day!❞

Beefed-Up Short Ribs

4 servings

prep: 35 minutes   cook: 9 hours

slow-cooker size: 4 quart

4   pounds lean beef short ribs
1   teaspoon salt
½   teaspoon pepper

1   (8-ounce) can tomato sauce
½   cup finely chopped celery
¼   cup finely chopped onion
2   tablespoons brown sugar
1   clove garlic, minced
⅛   teaspoon ground red pepper
3   tablespoons Worcestershire sauce
2   tablespoons lemon juice
2   tablespoons prepared mustard

1 Preheat the oven to 475°. Trim excess fat from ribs; sprinkle with salt and pepper. Place ribs on a lightly greased rack in a broiler pan. Bake at 475° for 30 minutes. Place ribs in a lightly greased 4-quart slow cooker.

2 Whisk together tomato sauce and next 8 ingredients in a small bowl; pour over ribs.

3 Cover and cook on LOW setting 9 hours. Skim excess fat from ribs before serving.

66 These beef short ribs cook slow, and are they ever easy and lip-smackin' good! I bake 'em first to bring out their flavor. See my tip on page 78 for degreasing the flavorful juices left in the slow cooker, then enjoy the home-cooked goodness of those juices over mashed potatoes or rice.99

Meaty Vegetable 'n' Rice Stuffed Peppers

(pictured on page 3)

6 servings

prep: 22 minutes   cook: 2 hours, 5 minutes

slow-cooker size: 7-quart oval

6	medium-sized red or green bell peppers
½	pound ground chuck
1	(10-ounce) package frozen seasoning blend
1	tablespoon fajita seasoning
2	teaspoons bottled minced garlic
1	(3½-ounce) bag boil-in-bag rice, uncooked
1	(14-ounce) can beef broth
1	cup (4 ounces) shredded sharp Cheddar cheese, divided
1	(26-ounce) jar fire-roasted tomato-and-garlic pasta sauce

1 Slice tops off peppers; remove seeds and veins. Rinse and drain peppers; stand them upright on a large, round microwave-safe platter. Microwave at HIGH 4 minutes or until barely crisp-tender. Cool slightly.

2 Meanwhile, cook beef and next 3 ingredients in a large skillet over medium-high heat, stirring until the beef crumbles and is no longer pink; drain and return beef mixture to skillet.

3 Cut top off bag of rice; stir rice into beef mixture, discarding bag. Stir in beef broth. Bring to a boil; reduce heat, and simmer, uncovered, 10 minutes. Remove from heat, and stir in ½ cup cheese.

4 Spoon about ½ cup beef mixture into each pepper. Place peppers in a single layer in a 7-quart oval slow cooker. Spoon pasta sauce over peppers.

5 Cover and cook on LOW setting 2 hours or until peppers are tender. Sprinkle peppers with remaining ½ cup cheese. Cover and cook on LOW setting 5 more minutes or until cheese melts.

66*Whet your appetite for Mexican flavors by digging into this filling meal of stuffed bell peppers. For added eye appeal, use red and green peppers (think of the Mexican flag). Olé!*99

No-Fuss Tacos

8 servings

prep: 7 minutes   cook: 5½ hours

slow-cooker size: 5 quart

1   large onion, sliced
1   (3- to 4-pound) sirloin beef roast,
        cut in half
1   (10-ounce) can diced tomatoes with
        lime juice and cilantro, undrained
2   tablespoons Mexican seasoning,
        divided

16   (6") flour tortillas
Toppings: shredded Cheddar cheese,
        sour cream, sliced scallions,
        shredded lettuce

1 Place onion in a 5-quart slow cooker; add roast and tomatoes. Sprinkle 1 tablespoon seasoning over top of roast.

2 Cover and cook on HIGH setting 5 hours. Remove roast, and shred with 2 forks; return to slow cooker, and stir in remaining 1 tablespoon seasoning. Cover and cook on HIGH setting 30 more minutes.

3 Heat tortillas according to package directions. Using a slotted spoon, spoon beef mixture evenly down centers of tortillas; top evenly with desired toppings, and roll up tightly.

66 *If the gang's running late—or just having too much fun—the meat for these tacos will hold for quite a while. Just switch the slow cooker to the WARM or LOW setting until everybody's ready to eat.* 99

Slow-Cooker Lasagna

(pictured on page 39)

6 to 8 servings

prep: 23 minutes   cook: 4 hours

slow-cooker size: 5 to 6 quart

1   pound ground round
½   pound hot Italian sausage, casings
          removed
1   medium onion, chopped

1   (15-ounce) container ricotta cheese
½   cup grated Parmesan cheese
½   teaspoon ground white pepper
¼   teaspoon garlic powder
1   (26-ounce) jar tomato-and-basil
          pasta sauce
⅓   cup water

8   lasagna noodles, uncooked
1   (8-ounce) package sliced fresh
          mushrooms
3   cups (12 ounces) shredded
          mozzarella cheese

1 Cook beef, sausage, and onion in a large skillet over medium-high heat, stirring until the meat crumbles and is no longer pink; drain.

2 Stir together ricotta and next 3 ingredients in a small bowl. In a separate bowl, combine pasta sauce and water.

3 Arrange 4 uncooked noodles in a lightly greased 5- to 6-quart slow cooker, breaking noodles as necessary to fit in slow cooker. Spoon half the meat mixture over noodles; top with half the sauce mixture and half the mushrooms. Spread ricotta mixture over mushrooms, and sprinkle with 1½ cups mozzarella cheese. Layer remaining noodles, beef mixture, sauce, mushrooms, and mozzarella cheese.

4 Cover and cook on LOW setting 4 hours or until noodles are done. Let stand 10 minutes before serving.

Forgive Me—NOT!

Most slow cooker recipes are very forgiving if allowed to cook beyond the time specified in the recipe. However, a lasagna recipe is an exception—don't let this dish cook longer than 4 hours or the noodles and cheese may begin to scorch.

Creamy Beef and Spinach

6 to 8 servings

prep: 35 minutes   cook: 5 hours

slow-cooker size: 4 quart

1   pound ground chuck
1   medium onion, chopped
1   (8-ounce) package sliced fresh
       mushrooms

1   (6-ounce) package fresh baby
       spinach
1   (14-ounce) can low-sodium fat-free
       beef broth
1   (10¾-ounce) can cream of
       mushroom soup, undiluted
1   (8-ounce) container sour cream
½   teaspoon salt
¼   teaspoon crushed red pepper
1   cup (8 ounces) crumbled feta
       cheese

Warm cooked egg noodles

1 Cook first 3 ingredients in a large skillet over medium heat, stirring until the beef crumbles and is no longer pink; drain.

2 Stir together beef mixture and spinach in a large skillet until spinach wilts, about 4 minutes. Add beef broth and next 5 ingredients to skillet. Spoon mixture into a lightly greased 4-quart slow cooker.

3 Cover and cook on LOW setting 5 hours. Serve over egg noodles.

"This is comfort food at its yummiest! Serve it as a one-dish meal, or round it out with a fresh fruit salad and rolls.**"**

Easy Cheesy Meat Loaf

6 to 8 servings

prep: 10 minutes   cook: 4 hours and 45 minutes

slow-cooker size: 3-quart oval

2   pounds ground round
1   cup ketchup, divided
1   (1½-ounce) package meat loaf
       seasoning
¾   cup fine, dry bread crumbs
       (store-bought)
2   large eggs
1   cup (4 ounces) shredded sharp
       Cheddar cheese

2   teaspoons prepared mustard

66 *I found an oval slow cooker works best to accommodate the shape of the meat loaf.* **99**

1 Combine beef, ½ cup ketchup, and next 4 ingredients in a large bowl; shape mixture in a 5"x7½" loaf. Place loaf in a lightly greased 3-quart oval slow cooker.

2 Cover and cook on HIGH setting 1 hour. Reduce heat to LOW setting, and cook 3 hours. Remove ceramic insert from cooker, and carefully pour grease off meat loaf; return insert to cooker.

3 Stir together remaining ½ cup ketchup and the mustard in a small bowl; spread over meat loaf. Cover and cook on LOW setting 45 more minutes or until thermometer inserted into meat loaf registers 160°. Remove meat loaf from slow cooker, and let stand 10 minutes before serving.

Smoky Barbecue Pork

19 servings

prep: 17 minutes   cook: 7 hours

slow-cooker size: 5 or 5½ quart

2	teaspoons dry mustard
1	teaspoon salt
½	teaspoon ground red pepper
1	(4- to 5-pound) boneless pork butt roast, cut in half
2	tablespoons butter
1	large onion, chopped
1	(16-ounce) bottle mesquite marinade
1	(19-ounce) bottle barbecue grilling sauce

1 Combine first 3 ingredients. Rub evenly over pork.

2 Melt butter in large nonstick skillet over medium-high heat. Add pork; cook 10 minutes or until browned on all sides.

3 Place onion and pork in a 5- or 5½-quart slow cooker. Add marinade and barbecue sauce.

4 Cover and cook on HIGH setting 7 hours or until pork is tender and shreds easily.

5 Remove pork to a large bowl, reserving sauce; shred pork with 2 forks. Pour sauce over shredded pork; stir well.

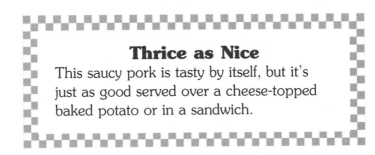

Thrice as Nice
This saucy pork is tasty by itself, but it's just as good served over a cheese-topped baked potato or in a sandwich.

Pork Tenderloin with Apples and Bacon

4 servings

prep: 18 minutes   cook: 6 hours

slow-cooker size: 5 quart

4	slices bacon
2	(¾-pound) pork tenderloins
2	medium-sized sweet onions, sliced
2	Braeburn apples, cored and cut into eighths
1	tablespoon dark brown sugar
1	teaspoon salt
½	teaspoon pepper
½	cup chicken broth
¼	cup apple cider vinegar

1 Cook bacon in a large skillet until crisp; remove and drain on paper towels, reserving 1 tablespoon drippings in skillet. Crumble bacon, and set aside. Brown pork in hot drippings 7 minutes or until browned.

2 Combine crumbled bacon, onions, and next 4 ingredients in a lightly greased 5-quart slow cooker. Place pork over apples and onions; pour broth and vinegar over pork.

3 Cover and cook on LOW setting 6 hours or until pork is tender.

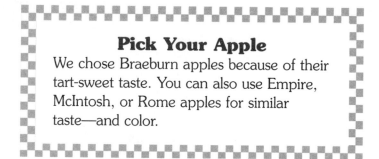

Pick Your Apple
We chose Braeburn apples because of their tart-sweet taste. You can also use Empire, McIntosh, or Rome apples for similar taste—and color.

Saucy Pork Ribs

6 servings

prep: 12 minutes   cook: 6 hours

slow-cooker size: 4 quart

4   pounds country-style pork ribs,
        trimmed
2   teaspoons salt, divided

¼   cup dried minced onion
1   cup packed brown sugar
1   (3.9-ounce) cup peach applesauce
1   cup ketchup
2   tablespoons orange marmalade
1   tablespoon steak sauce
1   teaspoon ground red pepper
1   teaspoon minced garlic
½   teaspoon Worcestershire sauce

1 Cut ribs apart; sprinkle 1 teaspoon salt evenly over ribs, and set aside.

2 Stir together remaining 1 teaspoon salt, the minced onion, and remaining 8 ingredients in a medium bowl until blended. Pour half of mixture into a 4-quart slow cooker. Place ribs in slow cooker, and pour remaining mixture over ribs.

3 Cover and cook on HIGH setting 6 hours or until meat almost falls off the bone.

66These sweet and saucy ribs have a kick, thanks to the ground red pepper. And they're fall-off-the bone tender!99

Farm-Style Pork Chops

7 servings

prep: 12 minutes   cook: 6 hours

slow-cooker size: 4 to 5 quart

1	(3-pound) boneless pork loin, trimmed
¼	cup soy sauce
¼	cup orange marmalade
2	tablespoons ketchup
1	clove garlic, pressed
2	tablespoons all-purpose flour

1 Cut pork into 1¼"-thick slices. Stir together soy sauce and next 3 ingredients; brush sauce over both sides of pork. Place pork in a 4- to 5-quart slow cooker, and pour remaining sauce over pork.

2 Cover and cook on HIGH setting 1 hour. Reduce to LOW setting, and cook 5 hours. Remove chops from slow cooker; keep warm.

3 Skim fat from sauce, and pour sauce into a small saucepan. Place saucepan over medium-high heat; whisk in flour. Bring to a boil; cook over medium-high heat for 4 minutes or until thickened. Serve over pork chops.

❝Serve up these savory pork chops tonight for a homestyle dinner with your family. They'll think you cooked all day. Take credit, and say you did!❞

Sausage-Florentine Manicotti

7 servings

prep: 20 minutes   cook: 2½ hours

slow-cooker size: 5 quart

4   quarts water
1   tablespoon salt
1   (8-ounce) package manicotti
       noodles, uncooked

1   (26-ounce) jar tomato-basil flavored
       pasta sauce
1   (10-ounce) package frozen chopped
       spinach, thawed and well drained

1   pound ground Italian sausage
1   (8-ounce) package cream cheese,
       softened
1   cup ricotta cheese
4   cups (16 ounces) shredded
       mozzarella cheese
¼   teaspoon salt
¼   teaspoon pepper
¼   cup chopped toasted walnuts
       (optional)

1 Bring water and salt to a boil in a large Dutch oven; add pasta. Cook for 5 minutes; drain and rinse with cold water.

2 Meanwhile, combine pasta sauce and spinach in a medium bowl; pour half the mixture into a lightly greased 5-quart slow cooker. Set remaining half of mixture aside.

3 Cook sausage in a large skillet over medium-high heat, stirring until meat crumbles and is no longer pink. Stir in cream cheese, ricotta cheese, 2 cups mozzarella cheese, the salt, pepper, and, if desired, walnuts. Spoon into manicotti shells (see tip); arrange stuffed shells in slow cooker. Pour reserved tomato mixture over shells; sprinkle with remaining 2 cups mozzarella cheese.

4 Cover and cook on LOW setting 2½ hours. Let stand 10 minutes.

Pasta Pointers

Try this no-hassle trick when stuffing manicotti shells: Slice the shell lengthwise, spoon the mixture evenly down the center of the shell, reshape, and then place cut side down in the slow cooker.

Cranberry Chicken

6 servings

prep: 9 minutes   cook: 7 hours and 15 minutes

slow-cooker size: 4 quart

1	small onion, thinly sliced
1	cup fresh or frozen cranberries
12	skinned and boned chicken thighs
¼	cup ketchup
2	tablespoons brown sugar
1	teaspoon dry mustard
½	teaspoon salt
2	teaspoons cider vinegar
1½	tablespoons cornstarch
2	tablespoons cold water

1 Combine onion and cranberries in a 4-quart slow cooker. Arrange chicken on top of cranberry mixture.

2 Combine ketchup and next 4 ingredients in a small bowl; pour over chicken.

3 Cover and cook on HIGH setting 1 hour; reduce heat to LOW setting, and cook 6 hours or until chicken is very tender. Transfer chicken to a serving platter, and keep warm.

4 Combine cornstarch and water, stirring until smooth; stir into mixture in slow cooker. Cook, uncovered, on HIGH setting 15 minutes or until mixture is slightly thickened, stirring often. Pour over chicken.

66 *Serve this sweet-and-sour chicken thigh combo over rice or noodles to soak up the oh-so-sassy sauce.* **99**

Polynesian Wings

4 to 6 servings

prep: 16 minutes   cook: 4 hours   marinate: 8 hours

slow-cooker size: 3 to 4 quart

2½ pounds chicken wings (about
     13 wings) (*see note*)

1   (11.5-ounce) can frozen orange-
     pineapple juice concentrate,
     thawed and undiluted
⅔   cup prepared peanut sauce
¼   cup minced fresh cilantro
2   teaspoons chili-garlic sauce
½   teaspoon bottled minced ginger
2   teaspoons orange marmalade

Wing Tip
Finishing these tasty wings in the slow cooker will ensure tender goodness with each savory bite. The slow cooker is also a good serving container that keeps the wings at an even temperature if you're having them at a party.

1 Cut off wing tips, and discard; cut wings in half at joint.

2 Combine juice concentrate and remaining 5 ingredients in a small bowl; reserve ¾ cup marinade, and chill remaining marinade. Pour reserved ¾ cup marinade into a large resealable plastic freezer bag; add chicken, and seal. Marinate in the refrigerator 8 hours, turning bag occasionally.

3 Remove chicken from marinade, discarding marinade. Place chicken skin-side up on a lightly greased rack in a broiler pan. Broil 3" from heat 8 minutes or until browned. Place wings in a 3- to 4-quart slow cooker.

4 Cover and cook on LOW setting 4 hours. Heat the chilled marinade thoroughly, and brush on wings just before serving.

Note: You can also buy chicken wings that have already been disjointed. You'll need 26 pieces.

Coconut Chicken Curry

4 to 6 servings

prep: 16 minutes   cook: 4 hours

slow-cooker size: 3 to 4 quart

1   tablespoon vegetable oil
3   (6-ounce) skinned and boned
       chicken breasts, cubed
1   (1-pound) package frozen pepper
       stir-fry mix
1½ teaspoons prepared minced garlic
1   teaspoon chicken bouillon granules
1   teaspoon ground ginger
2½ teaspoons curry powder
1   teaspoon salt

1   (14-ounce) can light coconut milk

4   cups warm cooked rice (see tip)
2   tablespoons chopped cilantro
¼   cup toasted slivered almonds
2   tablespoons sliced scallions

1 Heat vegetable oil in a large skillet over medium-high heat. Add chicken, and cook 8 minutes or until browned. Remove chicken from skillet, and place in a 3- to 4-quart slow cooker. Stir in pepper stir-fry mix and next 5 ingredients.

2 Cover and cook on HIGH setting 3½ hours. Stir in coconut milk; cover and cook on HIGH setting 30 more minutes.

3 Serve chicken mixture over rice; sprinkle with cilantro, almonds, and scallions.

Which Rice Is Right?

For a more traditional curry dish, substitute basmati rice for regular long-grain rice. Basmati rice is an aromatic long-grain rice that has a creamy yellow color and a distinctive perfumy, nutlike flavor and aroma.

Chipotle Chicken Enchilada Casserole

6 to 8 servings

prep: 22 minutes   cook: 2 hours and 15 minutes

slow-cooker size: 6 quart

2   tablespoons unsweetened cocoa
1   to 2 teaspoons chipotle chile
      powder
1   teaspoon garlic powder
2   (10-ounce) cans enchilada sauce
      (see tip)
3   cups shredded cooked chicken
3   cups (12 ounces) shredded
      Monterey Jack cheese, divided
14   (5½") corn tortillas

Toppings: chopped tomato, chopped
      avocado, sour cream, sliced
      scallions

1 Stir together first 4 ingredients in a medium bowl. Combine chicken, 2 cups cheese, and 1 cup enchilada sauce mixture in a large bowl. Spoon chicken mixture evenly down center of tortillas; roll up.

2 Pour ¾ cup enchilada sauce mixture in a 6-quart slow cooker; arrange enchiladas in layers over sauce, seam-side down. Pour remaining sauce over enchiladas.

3 Cover and cook on LOW setting 2 hours. Remove lid, and sprinkle with remaining 1 cup cheese. Cover and cook on LOW setting 15 more minutes or until cheese melts. Serve with desired toppings.

Tortilla Tidbit
Not all tortillas are created equal. So, don't be tempted to substitute flour tortillas for corn tortillas—the casserole will turn out too soggy.

Chicken 'n' Black Bean Burritos

6 servings

prep: 18 minutes   cook: 2 hours

slow-cooker: 5 to 6 quart

2 cups chopped cooked chicken
1 (1¼-ounce) package taco
    seasoning mix

1 (16-ounce) can refried black beans
6 (8") flour tortillas
2 cups (8 ounces) shredded Monterey
    Jack cheese
1 (10-ounce) can diced tomatoes and
    green chilies, drained

1 (8-ounce) container sour cream
2 tablespoons chopped fresh cilantro
1 tablespoon lime juice

1 Combine chicken and taco seasoning in a large resealable plastic freezer bag; seal bag, and shake to coat chicken.

2 Spread beans evenly down the center of tortillas; top evenly with chicken, cheese, and tomatoes. Fold bottom third of tortillas up and over filling, just until covered. Fold left and right sides of tortilla over, and roll up. Wrap each burrito in foil; arrange burritos in 2 layers in a 5- to 6-quart slow cooker. Cover and cook on HIGH setting 2 hours.

3 Meanwhile, stir together sour cream, cilantro, and lime juice in a small bowl. Cover and chill until ready to serve with burritos.

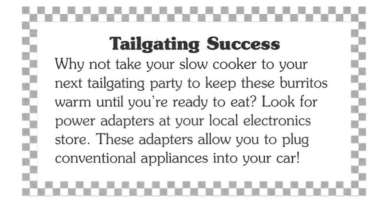

Tailgating Success

Why not take your slow cooker to your next tailgating party to keep these burritos warm until you're ready to eat? Look for power adapters at your local electronics store. These adapters allow you to plug conventional appliances into your car!

One-Dish Magic

> **"**One-dish meals and slow cookers go hand in hand in my book. Just prep and let 'em cook—then come back and enjoy!**"**

Mexican Cornbread-Stuffed Poblanos

5 servings

prep: 20 minutes   cook: 3 hours

slow-cooker size: 6-quart oval

5   large poblano chile peppers

¾   cup Mexican-style cornbread mix
      with jalapeño peppers

⅔   cup frozen chopped onion

1   (11-ounce) can whole kernel corn
      with sweet peppers, drained

1   cup (4 ounces) shredded Monterey
      Jack cheese with peppers

1   large egg, lightly beaten

¼   cup milk

1 Cut off top quarter of peppers, and discard. Remove and discard seeds and membranes to create shells. Rinse peppers, and drain. Place peppers cut side up in a circular pattern around the edge of a large round microwave-safe platter. Microwave at HIGH 2 minutes; drain.

2 Combine cornbread mix and remaining 5 ingredients in a medium bowl, stirring just until dry ingredients are moistened. Spoon cornbread mixture into peppers. Arrange peppers in a lightly greased 6-quart oval slow cooker.

3 Cover and cook on HIGH setting 3 hours.

One-Dish Delish!

This one-dish meal has it all. Your veggies, protein, and bread are all accounted for in one tasty serving. The only other ingredient you'll need is a cold drink!

Pizza-Style Macaroni

4 to 6 servings

prep: 10 minutes   cook: 4½ hours

slow-cooker size: 4 quart

1   (8-ounce) package elbow macaroni,
      uncooked
1   (14-ounce) jar pizza sauce
1   (10¾-ounce) can Cheddar cheese
      soup, undiluted
1   cup water
1   (8-ounce) package sliced pepperoni,
      chopped
1   large green bell pepper, chopped
1   (2.25-ounce) can sliced ripe olives,
      drained
2   teaspoons dried Italian seasoning
2   cups (8 ounces) shredded six-cheese
      Italian blend cheese, divided

1 Stir together first 8 ingredients in a large bowl; stir in 1½ cups cheese. Spoon mixture into a lightly greased 4-quart slow cooker; sprinkle with remaining ½ cup cheese.

2 Cover and cook on LOW setting 4½ hours or until macaroni is done.

This recipe combines two favorites: pizza and mac 'n' cheese! What's not to like about this winner?!

Creamy Shrimp 'n' Grits

(pictured on facing page)

6 servings

prep: 7 minutes   cook: 3½ hours

slow-cooker size: 5 quart

2   cups uncooked regular grits
2   (14-ounce) cans chicken broth
2   cups whipping cream
1   (10¾-ounce) can Cheddar cheese
     soup, undiluted
1   bunch scallions, chopped
3   tablespoons butter
2   teaspoons hot sauce
1   teaspoon salt

1   pound cooked, peeled, and
     deveined medium-sized shrimp
     (see tip)
Garnish: additional sliced scallions

1 Combine first 8 ingredients in a lightly greased 5-quart slow cooker.

2 Cover and cook on LOW setting 3 hours.

3 Remove lid; stir grits, and add shrimp. Cover and cook on LOW setting 30 more minutes. Garnish, if desired.

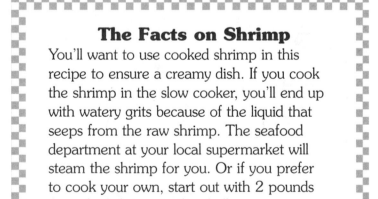

The Facts on Shrimp
You'll want to use cooked shrimp in this recipe to ensure a creamy dish. If you cook the shrimp in the slow cooker, you'll end up with watery grits because of the liquid that seeps from the raw shrimp. The seafood department at your local supermarket will steam the shrimp for you. Or if you prefer to cook your own, start out with 2 pounds uncooked shrimp in the shell.

Chorizo and Black Bean Chili,
page 68

Red Sauce and Meatballs,
page 155

Chipotle-Lime Pork Chops with Corn on the Cob

(pictured on facing page)

6 servings

prep: 16 minutes   cook: 4 hours

slow-cooker size: 5 to 6 quart

½ cup all-purpose flour
1½ teaspoons salt, divided
1 teaspoon pepper, divided
6 bone-in center-cut pork chops
 (about ½" thick)

2 to 3 tablespoons olive oil, divided

1 (12-ounce) bottle Baja chipotle
 marinade
¼ cup lime juice
2 scallions, sliced
1 cup barbecue sauce
4 large cloves garlic, pressed
3 ears fresh yellow corn, cut in half

1 Combine flour, 1 teaspoon salt, and ½ teaspoon pepper in a large resealable plastic freezer bag; add pork, tossing to coat.

2 Heat 1 tablespoon oil in a large nonstick skillet over medium-high heat. Cook pork, in batches, 2 minutes on each side or until browned, adding additional 1 tablespoon oil, if needed.

3 Place pork in a lightly greased 5- to 6-quart slow cooker. Combine marinade and next 3 ingredients; pour over pork in slow cooker. Rub remaining 1 tablespoon oil and the garlic evenly over corn. Sprinkle corn with remaining ½ teaspoon each of salt and pepper; add corn to slow cooker.

4 Cover and cook on LOW setting 4 hours or until meat is tender.

Nice 'n' Tender
The vinegar in the marinade tenderizes these juicy chops. And because the corn is cooked on top of the chops, you don't have to worry about it overcooking.

Fruity Pork Loin Pot Roast

8 servings

prep: 5 minutes   cook: 7 hours

slow-cooker size: 5 quart

3   tablespoons all-purpose flour
½   teaspoon salt
½   teaspoon pepper
1   (3½-pound) center-cut boneless
        pork loin roast

1   tablespoon olive oil
2   large sweet potatoes, peeled and cut
        into 1" slices
½   (10-ounce) package medium-sized
        pitted prunes
1   (6-ounce) package dried apricots
1   cup chicken broth
½   cup Madeira wine or beef broth
2   tablespoons brown sugar

1 Combine flour, salt, and pepper in a large resealable plastic freezer bag. Add pork, and shake to coat.

2 Heat oil in a large skillet over medium heat. Add pork, and cook until browned on all sides. Place browned pork in a 5-quart slow cooker. Arrange sweet potatoes, prunes, and apricots around pork. Combine broth, wine, and brown sugar; pour over pork.

3 Cover and cook on LOW setting 7 hours or until meat and sweet potatoes are tender. Let stand 10 minutes before serving.

66*The sweet potatoes and dried fruit turn this pork roast into a healthy one-dish meal—and that's good for everybody.***99**

Chalupa Dinner Bowl

8 servings

prep: 30 minutes   cook: 7 hours or 11 hours

slow-cooker size: 6 quart

1   pound dried pinto beans
1   (3½-pound) bone-in pork loin roast
2   (4.5-ounce) cans chopped green
      chilies
2   cloves garlic, chopped
1   tablespoon chili powder
2   teaspoons salt
1   teaspoon dried oregano
1   teaspoon ground cumin
1   (32-ounce) container chicken broth

1   (10-ounce) can diced tomatoes and
      green chilies with lime juice and
      cilantro

8   taco salad shells
1   small head iceberg lettuce, shredded
Toppings: shredded Monterey Jack
      cheese, pickled jalapeño slices,
      halved grape tomatoes, sour
      cream, chopped avocado

1 Rinse and sort beans according to package directions; place in a 6-quart slow cooker. Add roast and next 6 ingredients. Pour chicken broth over roast.

2 Cover and cook on HIGH setting 6 hours; or cook on HIGH setting 1 hour, reduce heat to LOW setting, and cook for 9 hours. Remove bones and fat from roast; pull roast into large pieces with 2 forks. Stir in diced tomatoes. Cook, uncovered, on HIGH setting 1 more hour or until liquid is slightly thickened.

3 Heat taco salad shells according to package directions; place shredded lettuce evenly into shells. Spoon about 1 cup pork-and-bean mixture into each shell, using a slotted spoon. Serve with desired toppings.

Muy Bien!

Chalupa is the Spanish word for "boat." It describes the taco shells that hold the savory pork-and-bean mixture. You can also serve the mixture over cornbread or rolled up burrito-style in flour tortillas.

Scalloped Potatoes with Ham

6 servings

prep: 20 minutes   cook: 8 hours

slow-cooker size: 5 quart

3	pounds medium potatoes, thinly sliced
1	medium onion, thinly sliced
1	cup diced cooked ham
1	cup (4 ounces) shredded American cheese (see tip)
½	teaspoon salt
¼	teaspoon pepper
1	(10¾-ounce) can cream of mushroom soup, undiluted
¾	cup water
1	tablespoon chopped fresh chives (optional)

1 Layer half each of first 4 ingredients in a 5-quart slow cooker. Sprinkle with salt and pepper; repeat layers with remaining potatoes, onion, ham, and cheese.

2 Stir together soup and ¾ cup water in a small bowl; spoon over potato mixture.

3 Cover and cook on LOW setting 7 to 8 hours. Sprinkle with chives, if desired.

Say Cheese!
I use American cheese in this slow-cooker version of scalloped potatoes for the smooth way it melts and coats these potatoes.

The Cheesiest Mac 'n' Cheese

6 servings

prep: 10 minutes   cook: 3½ hours

slow-cooker size: 3 to 4 quart

¼   cup all-purpose flour
1½ cups milk
2   teaspoons prepared mustard
1   teaspoon instant minced onion

1   (10¾-ounce) can Cheddar cheese
      soup, undiluted
1   (10-ounce) block sharp Cheddar
      cheese, shredded (see note)
1   (8-ounce) package pasteurized
      prepared cheese product, cubed
1   (8-ounce) package elbow macaroni,
      uncooked
1½ cups cubed cooked ham (optional)

1 Whisk together first 4 ingredients in a large bowl.

2 Combine milk mixture, soup, and remaining ingredients in a lightly greased 3- to 4-quart slow cooker.

3 Cover and cook on LOW setting 3½ hours. Let stand 10 minutes; stir before serving.

Note: You can also use 2½ cups of preshredded sharp Cheddar cheese.

Hot Tip

If you know your slow cooker has a "hot spot" on one side, try turning the crockery insert during the cook time to evenly distribute the heat. This will help prevent scorching or burning your food.

Cheesy Kielbasa with Beans

12 servings

prep: 20 minutes   cook: 10 hours

slow-cooker size: 5 quart

1   pound ground chuck
1   large green bell pepper, diced
1   large onion, chopped

1   (16-ounce) package kielbasa
     sausage, thinly sliced
2   (10¾-ounce) cans tomato soup,
     undiluted
1   (14½-ounce) can diced tomatoes,
     undrained
1   (10-ounce) can diced tomato and
     green chilies, undrained
4   (16-ounce) cans pinto beans,
     undrained
4   (15-ounce) cans pork and beans,
     undrained
½   teaspoon salt
½   teaspoon pepper

2   cups (8 ounces) shredded Cheddar
     cheese

1 Cook first 3 ingredients in a large skillet over medium-high heat, stirring until the beef crumbles and is no longer pink. Remove from skillet, and drain.

2 Brown sausage in skillet; drain. Place beef mixture, sausage, soup, and next 6 ingredients in a 5-quart slow cooker.

3 Cover and cook on LOW setting 8 to 10 hours. Stir in cheese just before serving.

Keen on Kielbasa

Sausage isn't just for breakfast anymore. Keep sausage, such as kielbasa, on hand for last-minute meals. It's precooked, easy to prepare, and a family favorite.

Red Beans and Rice

10 servings

prep: 6 minutes   cook: 4 hours

slow-cooker size: 4 quart

1¾ cups water
1   (16-ounce) package andouille
        sausage, sliced
1   (10-ounce) package frozen
        seasoning blend (see tip on
        page 128)
1   (14-ounce) can chicken broth
1   tablespoon Creole seasoning
1   tablespoon prepared minced garlic
1½ cups uncooked converted long-grain
        rice (see tip)

2   (15-ounce) cans red beans, rinsed
        and drained

1 Place first 7 ingredients in a 4-quart slow cooker; stir well.

2 Cover and cook on LOW setting 3½ hours. Stir in beans; cover and cook on HIGH setting 30 minutes or until beans are thoroughly heated. Let stand 10 minutes before serving.

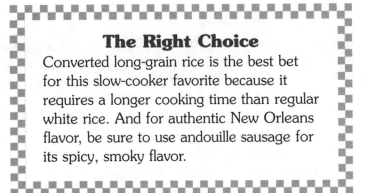

The Right Choice
Converted long-grain rice is the best bet for this slow-cooker favorite because it requires a longer cooking time than regular white rice. And for authentic New Orleans flavor, be sure to use andouille sausage for its spicy, smoky flavor.

Sausage and White Bean Cassoulet

6 servings

prep: 6 minutes   cook: 8 hours

slow-cooker size: 4 to 5 quart

2 (15.8-ounce) cans great Northern beans, undrained
1 (28-ounce) can diced tomatoes with garlic and onion, undrained
1 pound light smoked sausage, sliced
1 (10½-ounce) can French onion soup, undiluted
3 medium carrots, sliced
1 (1-ounce) package beef and herb gravy mix
2 teaspoons dried sage
½ teaspoon dried thyme

½ cup fine, dry bread crumbs (store-bought)
Freshly grated Parmesan cheese

1 Combine first 8 ingredients in a 4- to 5-quart slow cooker.

2 Cover and cook on LOW setting 8 hours or until carrots are tender. Stir in bread crumbs. Sprinkle each serving with Parmesan cheese.

ka-soo-LAY

Cassoulet is a French stew of white beans, sausage, pork, and goose or duck—the ingredient variation differs from region to region. It pairs well with a slow cooker because the traditional casserole is cooked slowly, covered, to blend the flavors.

Easy Burritos

8 to 10 servings

prep: 10 minutes   cook: 5½ hours

slow-cooker size: 5 quart

1   large onion, sliced into rings
1   (3- to 4-pound) sirloin beef roast
½   cup water
1   (1¼-ounce) package taco
        seasoning mix

1   (1¼-ounce) package taco
        seasoning mix

16   (6") flour tortillas
Toppings: diced tomatoes, diced onions,
        sliced jalapeño peppers, sour
        cream, black beans
4   cups (16 ounces) shredded Cheddar
        or Monterey Jack cheese
Salsa

1 Place onion rings in a 5-quart slow cooker; add roast and ½ cup water. Sprinkle 1 package taco seasoning mix over top of roast.

2 Cover and cook on HIGH setting 5 hours. Remove roast, and shred with 2 forks; return to slow cooker, and stir in remaining package of taco seasoning mix. Cover and cook on HIGH setting 30 more minutes or until boiling.

3 Heat tortillas according to package directions. Using a slotted spoon, spoon beef mixture evenly down center of each tortilla; top with desired toppings and then cheese. Roll up, and serve with salsa.

Ready When You Are
If the gang's not quite ready when the meat's done, turn your slow cooker to the WARM or LOW setting—this will hold for quite a while.

Hungarian Goulash

6 to 8 servings

prep: 15 minutes   cook: 6½ hours

slow-cooker size: 5 quart

2 pounds round steak (¾" thick), cut into ½" pieces
1 small onion, chopped
1 clove garlic, minced

2 tablespoons all-purpose flour
1 tablespoon paprika
1 teaspoon salt
½ teaspoon pepper
¼ teaspoon dried thyme
1 (28-ounce) can whole tomatoes, undrained and coarsely chopped
1 bay leaf

1 (8-ounce) container sour cream
Warm cooked buttered noodles or rice

1 Combine first 3 ingredients in a 5-quart slow cooker, stirring well.

2 Combine flour and next 4 ingredients in a small bowl, stirring well; add to meat mixture, tossing well to coat. Add tomatoes and bay leaf to meat mixture; stir well.

3 Cover and cook on HIGH setting 1 hour; reduce heat to LOW setting, and cook 5½ hours. **Remove and discard bay leaf.** Stir in sour cream. Serve over noodles or rice.

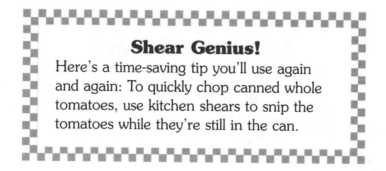

Shear Genius!

Here's a time-saving tip you'll use again and again: To quickly chop canned whole tomatoes, use kitchen shears to snip the tomatoes while they're still in the can.

Shepherd's Pie

11 servings

prep: 15 minutes   cook: 4 hours

slow-cooker size: 5½ to 6 quart

1   (22-ounce) package frozen mashed
        potatoes

1   pound ground round
2   tablespoons all-purpose flour

1   (10½-ounce) can French onion
        soup, undiluted
1   (16-ounce) package frozen vegetable
        mix, thawed

1   teaspoon salt
½   teaspoon pepper
½   cup (2 ounces) shredded sharp
        Cheddar cheese

1 Cook potatoes according to
microwave package directions.

2 Meanwhile, cook beef in a large skillet over medium-high heat 7 minutes, stirring until it crumbles and is no longer pink. Drain; stir in flour.

3 Add soup; cook, stirring constantly, 3 minutes or until slightly thickened. Stir in vegetable mix. Spoon mixture into a lightly greased 5½- or 6-quart slow cooker.

4 Add salt and pepper to potatoes. Spoon over beef mixture. Sprinkle with cheese.

5 Cover and cook on LOW setting 4 hours. Let stand 10 minutes before serving.

English History

Shepherd's pie is an old English dish traditionally made with ground lamb or mutton, vegetables, and gravy that's topped with mashed potatoes and then baked. I've updated this slow-cooker version by using ground beef and the convenience of frozen mashed potatoes and mixed vegetables.

Slow 'n' Easy Osso Bucco

4 servings

prep: 25 minutes   cook: 9 hours

slow-cooker size: 5 quart

2	tablespoons olive oil, divided
3	celery ribs, chopped
2	carrots, chopped
1	large onion, chopped
4	large cloves garlic, pressed
½	cup all-purpose flour
½	(1-ounce) package herb gravy mix for beef
½	teaspoon pepper
4	(1½"-thick) veal shanks (about 3 pounds)
½	teaspoon salt
1	(14½-ounce) can diced tomatoes with balsamic vinegar, basil, and oil
1	(10½-ounce) can beef consommé
¾	teaspoon dried rosemary
¼	teaspoon dried thyme
4	cups cooked polenta

1 Heat 1 tablespoon oil in a large non-stick skillet over medium-high heat. Add celery and next 3 ingredients; sauté 3 minutes or until tender. Transfer vegetables to a 5-quart slow cooker.

2 Combine flour, gravy mix, and pepper in a large shallow dish. Sprinkle veal shanks with salt; dredge veal shanks in flour mixture.

3 Heat remaining 1 tablespoon oil in skillet. Add veal shanks; cook 3 to 4 minutes on each side or until browned. Place shanks on top of vegetables in slow cooker. Add tomatoes and next 3 ingredients.

4 Cover and cook on LOW setting 9 hours or until tender. Serve veal with sauce over polenta.

"Traditionally, this Italian dish is served with risotto, but I like the convenient option of instant polenta. You can find it either with the grains or with the rice and pasta at your local supermarket. It's ooh so easy—and good!"

Grillades and Grits

4 to 6 servings

prep: 15 minutes   cook: 5 hours or 8 hours

slow-cooker size: 4 to 5 quart

2   tablespoons vegetable oil
2   tablespoons all-purpose flour

1½ pounds top round steak
1   (14½-ounce) can diced tomatoes,
        undrained
1   cup chopped onion
½   cup chopped green bell pepper
3   cloves garlic, pressed
1   tablespoon chopped fresh parsley
1½ teaspoons salt
½   teaspoon dried oregano
¼   teaspoon ground red pepper
¼   teaspoon freshly ground black
        pepper

Warm cooked grits

1 Heat oil in a small skillet over medium heat; whisk in flour. Cook, stirring constantly, 5 minutes or until roux is caramel colored; place in a 4- to 5-quart slow cooker.

2 Add steak and next 9 ingredients to slow cooker.

3 Cover and cook on HIGH setting 4 to 5 hours; or cook on HIGH setting 1 hour, reduce heat to LOW setting, and cook for 7 hours. Remove meat from slow cooker, and shred with 2 forks; return meat to slow cooker, stirring to blend. Spoon over grits.

"Grillade *is the French term for grilled or broiled food. It's cooked in a rich, seasoned sauce with tomatoes and other vegetables. This classic Creole dish is* most popular served for a brunch, but it's just as good as a dinner option, too!"

Chicken 'n' Rice Dinner

5 servings

prep: 8 minutes   cook: 6 hours

slow-cooker size: 5 to 6 quart

5   large skinned and boned chicken
      breasts (about 9 ounces each)
1   (14-ounce) can chicken broth
1   (10¾-ounce) can cream of chicken
      soup, undiluted
1   (4.5-ounce) can chopped green
      chilies, undrained
1   medium onion, chopped
1   teaspoon salt
½   teaspoon pepper

Warm cooked rice

1 Place chicken in a 5- to 6-quart slow cooker. Stir together broth and next 5 ingredients in a medium bowl; pour over chicken.

2 Cover and cook on HIGH setting 1 hour; reduce heat to LOW setting, and cook 5 hours. Serve chicken and sauce over rice.

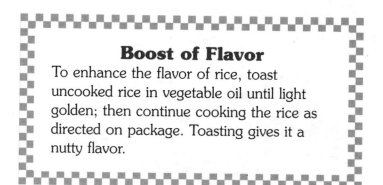

Boost of Flavor

To enhance the flavor of rice, toast uncooked rice in vegetable oil until light golden; then continue cooking the rice as directed on package. Toasting gives it a nutty flavor.

Bow-tie Pasta and Chicken Casserole

6 to 8 servings

prep: 18 minutes   cook: 4 hours

slow-cooker size: 5 quart

1   (10-ounce) package frozen chopped
       spinach, thawed
2   cups chopped cooked rotisserie
       chicken
1   (10¾-ounce) can cream of chicken
       and mushroom soup, undiluted
1   (10¾-ounce) can cream of celery
       soup, undiluted
1   (8-ounce) container sour cream
1   cup milk
1   (8-ounce) package sliced fresh
       mushrooms, chopped
½   teaspoon pepper
½   teaspoon salt
2   (8-ounce) packages shredded Italian
       three-cheese blend

16   ounces bow-tie (farfalle) pasta,
       uncooked
1   cup freshly shredded Parmesan
       cheese
½   cup toasted walnuts, chopped

1 Drain spinach well, pressing between
paper towels to remove excess mois-
ture. Stir together spinach, chicken, and
next 7 ingredients in a large bowl; stir in
1 package of cheese blend.

2 Arrange ⅓ of the uncooked noodles
in a lightly greased 5-quart slow
cooker. Spread ¼ of the chicken
mixture over noodles, and sprinkle with
⅔ cup cheese blend; repeat layers. Top
with remaining noodles, chicken mixture,
and cheese blend. Sprinkle top with
Parmesan cheese and walnuts.

3 Cover and cook on LOW setting
3½ to 4 hours or until noodles are
done. Let stand 10 minutes before serving.

❝I like this dish not only
because it's great tasting,
but also because you don't
have to precook the pasta. That's what I
call hands-off cooking!❞

Mama's Cheesy Chicken 'n' Broccoli Casserole

8 servings

prep: 18 minutes   cook: 5 hours

slow-cooker size: 5 quart

8   ounces wide egg noodles

3   cups (12 ounces) shredded sharp
       Cheddar cheese, divided
1   medium onion, finely chopped
1   (10-ounce) package frozen broccoli
       florets
3   cups chopped cooked chicken
1   (10¾-ounce) can cream of chicken
       soup, undiluted
1   (8-ounce) container sour cream
½   cup milk
½   teaspoon salt
½   teaspoon pepper

1   cup crushed round buttery crackers
       (about 20)

1 Prepare noodles according to package directions. Drain.

2 Combine noodles, 2 cups cheese, and next 8 ingredients in a large bowl, stirring well. Spoon into a lightly greased 5-quart slow cooker.

3 Cover and cook on LOW setting 4½ hours.

4 Combine remaining 1 cup cheese and the cracker crumbs. Uncover slow cooker, tilting lid so condensation runs back into casserole. Sprinkle crumb mixture over casserole. Cover and cook on LOW setting 30 more minutes.

Note: Carefully remove lid at end of cooking so condensation doesn't run into casserole and make the crumbs soggy.

Kick It Up!

Add a Southwestern flair to this casserole by substituting condensed Cheddar cheese soup and Cheddar cheese with habañero peppers for the cream of chicken soup and sharp Cheddar cheese.

Chicken Cobbler Pie

6 servings

prep: 12 minutes   cook: 6 hours

slow-cooker size: 4 to 5 quart

1   (16-ounce) package frozen mixed
     vegetables (see tip)
1   (10¾-ounce) can cream of chicken
     soup, undiluted
1   (10¾-ounce) can cream of potato
     soup, undiluted
2   cups chopped cooked chicken
1   cup milk
¼   teaspoon poultry seasoning
¼   teaspoon pepper

1½ cups biscuit mix
1   tablespoon sugar
3   tablespoons butter
1   (8-ounce) container sour cream

1 Combine first 7 ingredients in a 4- to 5-quart slow cooker.

2 Combine biscuit mix and sugar. Cut in butter with a pastry blender or 2 forks until crumbly; add sour cream, stirring until dry ingredients are moistened and a soft dough forms. Drop dough by large spoonfuls on top of chicken mixture.

3 Cover and cook on LOW setting 6 hours or until topping is lightly browned.

66*There are dozens of frozen mixed vegetable combinations found in the freezer section of your grocer. For this comfort food classic, I like the mix containing carrots, corn, green beans, peas, and lima beans.*99

Braised Chicken Thighs Dinner

3 to 6 servings

prep: 15 minutes   cook: 7 hours

slow-cooker size: 6-quart round

1   medium onion, halved lengthwise
      and sliced
4   medium-sized new potatoes (about
      1 pound), cut into ¼"-thick slices
2   cups baby carrots
1¼ teaspoons salt, divided
½   teaspoon pepper, divided
¼   cup chicken broth
¼   cup dry white wine (see tip)
1   teaspoon minced garlic
½   teaspoon dried thyme
1   teaspoon paprika
6   bone-in, skinned chicken thighs
      (about 1½ to 1¾ pounds)

1 Place onion in a lightly greased 6-quart round slow cooker; top with potatoes and carrots. Combine ¾ teaspoon salt, ¼ teaspoon pepper, the broth, and next 3 ingredients. Pour broth mixture over vegetables. Combine paprika, remaining ½ teaspoon salt, and remaining ¼ teaspoon pepper; rub evenly over chicken thighs, and arrange over vegetables.

2 Cover and cook on HIGH setting 1 hour; reduce heat to LOW setting, and cook 6 hours or until chicken and vegetables are tender.

I like the diversity of this one-dish winner. First, because it's a change from roast. Second, because it uses chicken thighs—they have so much more flavor than breasts. Feel free to substitute an extra ¼ cup chicken broth in place of the wine, if you prefer.

Turkey and Rice Casserole

8 servings

prep: 10 minutes   cook: 4 hours

slow-cooker size: 5 quart

2   (10¾-ounce) cans cream of
      mushroom soup, undiluted
3   cups water
2   cups uncooked converted long-grain
      white rice
1   cup thinly sliced celery
3   cups chopped cooked turkey
2   cups frozen mixed vegetables
1   teaspoon poultry seasoning
1   tablespoon dried minced onion
1   teaspoon dried oregano
1   teaspoon salt
½   teaspoon pepper

1 Combine soup and water in a 5-quart slow cooker. Add rice and remaining ingredients, and stir well.

2 Cover and cook on LOW setting 3½ to 4 hours or until most of the liquid is absorbed. Stir well before serving.

Leftover Trick

You can freeze leftovers in a baking dish for up to 1 month. When ready to serve, thaw casserole, and sprinkle with crushed round buttery crackers; then bake at 350° for 30 minutes or until warmed through.

Loaded Jambalaya Stew

7 servings

prep: 15 minutes   cook: 5 hours and 15 minutes

slow-cooker size: 5 quart

1½ pounds skinned and boned chicken
    thighs, cut into 1" pieces
1   tablespoon Creole seasoning

2   tablespoons vegetable oil

1   (10-ounce) package frozen
    seasoning blend, thawed (see tip)
1   (14½-ounce) can diced tomatoes
    with jalapeños, undrained
1   (8-ounce) package cubed ham
1   (14-ounce) can seasoned chicken
    broth with roasted garlic

2   (3.5-ounce) bags boil-in-bag rice
1   pound medium-sized fresh shrimp,
    peeled and deveined
½   cup chopped scallions
1   tablespoon hot sauce

1 Sprinkle chicken evenly with Creole seasoning.

2 Heat oil in a large skillet over high heat. Add chicken, and cook 4 to 5 minutes or until browned, stirring occasionally. Spoon chicken into a 5-quart slow cooker.

3 Add seasoning blend and next 3 ingredients to slow cooker. Cover and cook on LOW setting 5 hours.

4 Cook rice according to package directions. Stir cooked rice, shrimp, scallions, and hot sauce into stew. Increase heat to HIGH setting, cover, and cook 15 minutes or until shrimp turn pink.

Loaded Convenience

You won't waste time chopping veggies for this dish. We use a frozen seasoning blend that contains chopped onions, celery, green and red bell peppers, and parsley.

5 Ingredients or Less

> **"**Great food with just 5 ingredients? You betcha! And just so you know, I don't count salt, pepper, or water as part of the five, since most people have 'em on hand.**"**

Cajun Boiled Peanuts

18 cups

prep: 3 minutes   cook: 18 hours

slow-cooker size: 5 to 6 quart

2   pounds raw peanuts, in shell
¾   cup salt
12   cups water
1   (3-ounce) package boil-in-bag
        shrimp and crab boil
⅓   to ½ cup hot sauce

1 Combine all ingredients in a 5- to 6-quart slow cooker.

2 Cover and cook on HIGH setting 18 hours or until peanuts are soft. Drain peanuts before serving or storing. Store in resealable plastic freezer bags in the refrigerator up to 2 weeks.

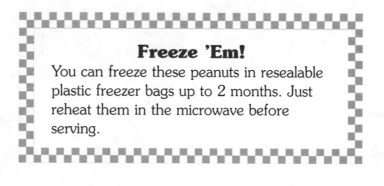

Freeze 'Em!

You can freeze these peanuts in resealable plastic freezer bags up to 2 months. Just reheat them in the microwave before serving.

French Dip Sandwiches

(pictured on page 38)

12 servings

prep: 5 minutes   cook: 9 hours

slow-cooker size: 4 to 5 quart

1   (3½- to 4-pound) boneless chuck
    roast, trimmed
2   tablespoons soy sauce
1   (1.6-ounce) package garlic herb
    sauce mix
2   (14-ounce) cans low-sodium beef
    broth

12 (3.3-ounce) French sandwich rolls,
    split and toasted

1 Cut roast in half; place in a 4- to 5-quart slow cooker. Stir together soy sauce, sauce mix, and broth in a medium bowl; pour over roast.

2 Cover and cook on HIGH setting 1 hour. Reduce heat to LOW setting, and cook 8 hours.

3 Remove beef from slow cooker, reserving broth. Shred beef with 2 forks. Spoon beef evenly over toasted rolls, and serve with reserved broth.

66 *The next time you're having the gang over to watch the game, serve these savory sandwiches. They're the perfect no-fuss solution for feeding a hungry crowd.* 99

Melt-in-Your-Mouth Roast

8 servings

prep: 16 minutes   cook: 7 hours and 15 minutes

slow-cooker size: 3½ or 4 quart

1   large onion, sliced and separated
      into rings

1   (3- to 3½-pound) bottom round
      roast
2   teaspoons salt
½   teaspoon pepper
1   tablespoon vegetable oil

½   cup water, divided
2   tablespoons Worcestershire sauce

3   tablespoons all-purpose flour

66*This roast really lives up
to its name! It gets its rich
flavor from just a few simple
ingredients. Be sure to cut the roast in half
before placing it in the slow cooker, to
ensure even cooking.*99

1 Place onion rings in a 3½- or 4-quart
slow cooker.

2 Trim excess fat from roast, and cut in
half crosswise. Combine salt and
pepper, and rub on all sides of roast.
Heat oil in a large skillet over medium-
high heat; add roast, and cook 10 minutes or until dark brown on all sides,
turning occasionally. Place roast on top
of onion rings in slow cooker.

3 Add ¼ cup water and the
Worcestershire sauce to skillet, stirring to loosen particles from bottom of
skillet. Pour sauce mixture over meat
and onions.

4 Cover and cook on LOW setting
7 hours or until meat is very tender.
Remove meat to a platter; cover and
keep warm.

5 Whisk remaining ¼ cup water into
the flour in a small bowl until smooth.
Whisk flour mixture into onions and drippings in cooker. Increase heat to HIGH
setting; cover and cook 15 minutes or
until bubbly and thickened. Serve onion
gravy over roast.

Easy Barbecue Pork

6 servings

prep: 5 minutes   cook: 8 hours

slow-cooker size: 5 to 6 quart

1   (3- to 4-pound) shoulder pork roast
1   (18-ounce) bottle barbecue sauce
1   (12-ounce) can cola soft drink

1 Place pork roast in a 5- to 6-quart slow cooker; pour barbecue sauce and cola over roast.

2 Cover and cook on HIGH setting 8 hours or until meat is tender and shreds easily. Remove pork from sauce, and shred with 2 forks. Stir pork into sauce.

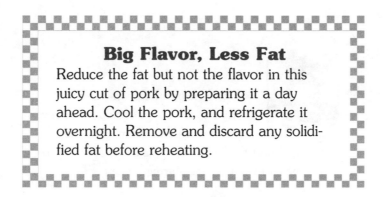

Big Flavor, Less Fat

Reduce the fat but not the flavor in this juicy cut of pork by preparing it a day ahead. Cool the pork, and refrigerate it overnight. Remove and discard any solidified fat before reheating.

Sweet 'n' Citrusy Pork Chops

6 servings

prep: 8 minutes   cook: 4 hours

slow-cooker size: 4 to 5 quart

6   (¾"-thick) center-cut pork loin
    chops, trimmed
1   teaspoon salt
1   teaspoon pepper

¼   cup packed light brown sugar
¾   cup orange juice
2   cloves garlic, minced
2   medium oranges, unpeeled and
    sliced

1 Sprinkle pork chops on both sides with salt and pepper. Place chops in a 4- to 5-quart slow cooker.

2 Combine brown sugar, orange juice, and garlic in a small bowl; pour over chops. Arrange orange slices over chops.

3 Cover and cook on HIGH setting 1 hour. Reduce heat to LOW setting, and cook 3 hours.

*66 These chops are fall-off-the-bone good! The long, slow cooking tenderizes them so much that the meat literally starts to fall off the bone. Serve the chops over rice to enjoy the gravy that's made during cooking.*99

Slow-Roasted Chicken with White Wine Jus

4 servings

prep: 24 minutes   cook: 5 hours

slow-cooker size: 6 quart

1   (5- to 6-pound) whole chicken
1   (1-ounce) package Ranch seasoning
        mix
¼   cup olive oil

¼   cup dry white wine or chicken broth
1   tablespoon white balsamic vinegar

66 *Forget the preroasted chicken from the deli! With a minimum amount of prep time, this version is just as convenient. Plus, you get all the tasty 'au jus' to serve over your chicken and side dish.* 99

1 Cut chicken in half lengthwise. Stir together seasoning mix and oil; rub chicken with oil mixture.

2 Place chicken halves breast side down in a 6-quart slow cooker. Cover and cook on HIGH setting 1 hour. Reduce heat to LOW setting, and cook 4 hours or until done. Remove chicken from slow cooker, reserving drippings.

3 Place a resealable plastic freezer bag inside a 2-cup glass measuring cup. Pour drippings into bag; let stand 10 minutes (fat will rise to the top). Seal bag; carefully snip off 1 bottom corner of bag. Drain drippings into a small saucepan, stopping before fat layer reaches opening; discard fat and bag. Add wine and vinegar to saucepan; bring to a boil. Reduce heat; simmer 10 minutes. Serve over chicken.

Creamy Lemon-Pepper Turkey Breast over Rice

6 servings

prep: 5 minutes   cook: 6 hours

slow-cooker size: 5 quart

1   (5-pound) bone-in turkey breast, cut
       in half
1   teaspoon salt
2   teaspoons lemon-pepper

2   tablespoons all-purpose flour
3   tablespoons water
Warm cooked rice

1 Sprinkle turkey evenly with salt and lemon-pepper. Place turkey breast halves meaty sides down in a 5-quart slow cooker.

2 Cover and cook on HIGH setting 1 hour; reduce heat to LOW setting, and cook 5 hours or until turkey is tender. Remove turkey from slow cooker, reserving juices in slow cooker; set turkey aside, and keep warm.

3 Combine flour and water in a medium saucepan, stirring with a whisk until well blended; gradually stir in reserved juices from slow cooker. Bring mixture to a boil over medium-high heat, stirring constantly. Reduce heat, and simmer 4 minutes or until thickened, stirring occasionally. Serve gravy over turkey with warm cooked rice.

"Consider this incredibly moist turkey breast for your next holiday meal. It'll free up your oven for making more goodies—such as homemade pie! I suggest having the butcher cut the turkey breast in half to ensure even cooking.**"**

Creamy Corn for a Crowd

10 to 12 servings

prep: 5 minutes   cook: 4 hours

slow-cooker size: 4 to 5 quart

2	(1-pound, 12-ounce) bags frozen whole kernel corn
2	tablespoons sugar
6	tablespoons water
1	(8-ounce) package cream cheese
½	cup butter

1 Place corn in a 4- to 5-quart slow cooker. Sprinkle corn with sugar, and drizzle with water. Place cream cheese and butter on top of corn mixture (do not stir).

2 Cover and cook on LOW setting 4 hours. Stir well before serving.

66*This potluck pleaser is a breeze to make and feeds a crowd! Don't be surprised that the cream cheese still retains its block shape after 4 hours of cooking—it's very soft and blends easily when stirred.*99

Burgundy Mushrooms

10 servings

prep: 5 minutes   cook: 5 hours or 10 hours

slow-cooker size: 6 quart

3   pounds fresh button mushrooms
1½ cups Burgundy wine
1   (10½-ounce) can French onion
       soup
½   cup butter, cut into pieces
2   teaspoons balsamic vinegar
½   teaspoon salt
¼   teaspoon black pepper

1 Place mushrooms in a 6-quart slow cooker; add wine and remaining ingredients.

2 Cover and cook on HIGH setting 5 hours or on LOW setting 8 to 10 hours. Serve with a slotted spoon.

66These little gems are just the right choice to serve as a side with grilled steak. The gang will love 'em!99

Caramelized Onions

2 cups

prep: 10 minutes   cook: 4 hours

slow-cooker size: 3 to 4 quart

2   slices bacon

2   tablespoons butter, melted
2   medium-sized sweet onions, sliced
     (about 4½ cups)
¼   teaspoon salt
⅛   teaspoon pepper

1 Cook bacon in a skillet until crisp; remove bacon, reserving 1 table-spoon drippings. Reserve bacon for another use.

2 Combine reserved drippings, melted butter, and remaining 3 ingredients in a 3- to 4-quart slow cooker. Stir well to coat onions.

3 Cover and cook on HIGH setting 4 hours.

So Many Choices!
These savory onions are great served as a side dish for grilled steak or chicken, piled on roast beef sandwiches, or used as a pizza topping. I don't recommend cooking them on the LOW setting—you need the high heat to caramelize them.

Italian Zucchini and Tomatoes

8 servings

prep: 7 minutes   cook: 3 hours

slow-cooker size: 3½ or 4 quart

2   (14½-ounce) cans diced tomatoes
    with basil, garlic, and oregano
2   pounds zucchini, cut into ¼" slices
    (about 4 large)
1   medium-sized green bell pepper,
    sliced into 2" strips
¼   teaspoon freshly ground black
    pepper
2   tablespoons dried minced onion

Grated Parmesan cheese (optional)

1 Drain 1 can of tomatoes. Stir together drained tomatoes, the remaining can of undrained tomatoes, the zucchini, and next 3 ingredients in a 3½- or 4-quart slow cooker.

2 Cover and cook on HIGH setting 3 hours. Serve with a slotted spoon or, to enjoy the juices, serve in small bowls. Sprinkle with cheese, if desired.

That's Italian!
Top these veggies with other Italian cheeses, such as Parmigiano-Reggiano, an aged cheese with a complex, sharp flavor. Or try Romano, which has a sharp, tangy, and slightly salty flavor.

Maple-Honey Applesauce

8 servings

prep: 13 minutes   cook: 4 hours

slow-cooker size: 5 to 6 quart

12 large Granny Smith apples (about
    5½ pounds)
¼   cup lemon juice
½   cup sugar
½   cup pure maple syrup
½   cup honey

1 Peel, core, and cut apples into 1½" chunks. Place in a large bowl. Stir in lemon juice and remaining ingredients. Place mixture in a 5- to 6-quart slow cooker.

2 Cover and cook on HIGH setting 4 hours. Stir until desired consistency. Store in an airtight container in the refrigerator up to 1 week.

66Once you try this applesauce, you'll never go back to the store-bought version—I guarantee! Be sure to use pure maple syrup, 'cause pancake syrup just won't do in here.99

Warm Brownie Sundaes

10 servings

prep: 5 minutes   cook: 4 hours   stand: 30 minutes

slow-cooker size: 3 quart

1   (19.8-ounce) package dark
       chocolate fudge brownie mix
¾   cup butter, melted
½   cup sugar
6   large eggs, lightly beaten

1   pint vanilla ice cream

1 Stir together first 4 ingredients in a large bowl. Pour into a lightly greased 3-quart slow cooker.

2 Cover and cook on LOW setting 4 hours or until brownie pulls away from edge of cooker and center still jiggles. Unplug cooker; let stand, covered, 30 minutes. Serve warm with ice cream.

Talk about decadent—this dessert is the hands-down winner! Topped with your favorite ice cream, this gooey, fudgy brownie treat will have 'em beggin' for more.

Caramel Fondue

18 servings

prep: 12 minutes   cook: 3½ hours

slow-cooker size: 3 quart

2   (14-ounce) packages caramels, unwrapped
2   (14-ounce) cans sweetened condensed milk

Apple slices
Pound cake squares

1 Place caramels in a 3-quart slow cooker; stir in condensed milk.

2 Cover and cook on LOW setting 3½ hours until caramels melt and mixture is smooth, stirring occasionally. Serve with apple slices and pound cake squares.

Dual Purpose
Your slow cooker does double duty as a fondue pot, keeping this sweet mixture at the perfect temperature for easy dipping. If there's any fondue left over, reheat it in the microwave at 1-minute intervals until heated through.

Oh-So-Easy Caramel Pie

8 servings

prep: 5 minutes   cook: 4½ hours

slow-cooker size: 1 or 1½ quart

2   (14-ounce) cans sweetened
    condensed milk

1   (6-ounce) ready-made graham
    cracker crust

1   (8-ounce) container frozen whipped
    topping, thawed

1   (1.4-ounce) chocolate-covered toffee
    candy bar, coarsely chopped

1 Pour condensed milk into a 1- or
  1½-quart slow cooker.

2 Cover and cook 4½ hours or until
  condensed milk is the color of peanut
  butter, stirring mixture with a wire whisk
  every 30 minutes.

3 Pour caramel into graham cracker
  crust; cool. Spread whipped topping
  over top, and sprinkle with chopped
  candy bar. Cover and chill.

No Substitutes, Please

If you don't own a 1- or 1½-quart slow
cooker, you'll want to borrow one or pick
one up to make this wildly delicious recipe.
Just don't try it in a larger slow cooker or
be tempted to skip stirring it every 30 minutes—the caramel will scorch easily. There's
no HIGH or LOW setting on these size
cookers—only GO!

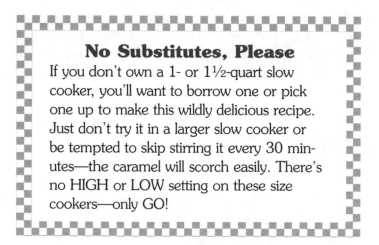

Living Light

66 *Slow and light meals are what I like to keep up my trimmed-down physique! Flavor's not sacrificed here—just the fat and calories.* 99

Mulled Pomegranate Punch

6 cups

prep: 4 minutes   cook: 3 hours

slow-cooker size: 3 to 4 quart

4   cups pomegranate juice
2   cups apple juice
8   large whole allspice
1   (3") stick cinnamon
¼   cup packed light brown sugar
12   black peppercorns

2   teaspoons lime juice

1 Combine first 6 ingredients in a 3- to 4-quart slow cooker.

2 Cover and cook on LOW setting 3 hours. Stir in lime juice. Pour mixture though a wire-mesh strainer into a pitcher.

Per ½-cup serving: CALORIES 86 (1% from fat); FAT 0.1g (sat 0g, mono 0g, poly 0g); PROTEIN 0.5g; CARBOHYDRATE 21.6g; FIBER 0.1g; CHOLESTEROL 0mg; IRON 0.3mg; SODIUM 13mg; CALCIUM 23mg

Had Your Pomegranate Juice Lately?

Pomegranate juice is gaining popularity not only for its great taste but also for its many health benefits, including being rich in antioxidants. So in addition to warming your body as you sip on this mulled punch, you're gaining healthy benefits.

Vegetable-Chickpea Curry

8 servings

prep: 5 minutes   cook: 6 hours

slow-cooker size: 5 quart

1   (6.7-ounce) package garlic-basil rice
3   carrots, cut into ¼" pieces
2   (15½-ounce) cans chickpeas, rinsed
      and drained
1   (10-ounce) package frozen
      seasoning blend
1   cup fresh green beans, cut into
      1" pieces
1   (14.5-ounce) can diced tomatoes
      and zesty green chilies, undrained
1   (14-ounce) can vegetable broth
2   teaspoons curry powder

1   (10-ounce) package frozen chopped
      spinach, thawed and drained
1   (13.5-ounce) can light coconut milk

1 Remove seasoning packet from rice
 package. Combine seasoning packet,
carrots, and next 6 ingredients in a
5-quart slow cooker.

2 Cover and cook on LOW setting
 5 hours. Stir in spinach, coconut
milk, and rice. Increase heat to HIGH
setting; cover and cook 1 hour or until
mixture is thoroughly heated and rice is
tender.

Per serving: CALORIES 238 (13% from fat); FAT 3.5g (sat 2.3g, mono 0.2g, poly 0.5g); PROTEIN 8.8g; CARBOHYDRATE 44.8g; FIBER 6.11g; CHOLESTEROL 0mg; IRON 2.4mg; SODIUM 704mg; CALCIUM 104mg

"*Entice your family with the taste of the Far East as the tantalizing aroma of this slow-cooked Indian dish fills your home.***"**

Salmon with Creamy Herb Sauce

4 servings

prep: 11 minutes   cook: 2 hours and 45 minutes

slow-cooker size: 5-quart oval

¼   cup vertically sliced small onion
2   lemons, sliced
10   black peppercorns
2   bay leaves
1   cup fat-free, less-sodium chicken
        broth
1   cup dry white wine or fat-free,
        less-sodium chicken broth

4   (6-ounce) skinless salmon fillets
        (about 1" thick)
½   teaspoon garlic salt
¼   teaspoon crushed red pepper

¼   cup light mayonnaise
⅛   cup reduced-fat sour cream
1   tablespoon chopped fresh parsley
½   tablespoon chopped fresh dill
1   teaspoon Dijon mustard
½   teaspoon fresh lemon juice
⅛   teaspoon freshly ground black
        pepper

1 Place first 4 ingredients in a 5-quart oval slow cooker; add chicken broth and wine.

2 Cover and cook on HIGH setting 2 hours. Meanwhile, sprinkle salmon with garlic salt and red pepper; cover and chill.

3 Stir together mayonnaise and remaining 6 ingredients in a small bowl; cover and chill herb sauce.

4 Place salmon on top of shallots and lemon slices; cook on HIGH setting 30 to 45 more minutes or until desired degree of doneness. Carefully transfer salmon to a serving platter, using a large spatula. Serve with creamy herb sauce.

Per serving (1 fillet plus 1½ tablespoons sauce): CALORIES 380 (58% from fat); FAT 24.4g (sat 5.3g, mono 6.9g, poly 6.7g); PROTEIN 35g; CARBOHYDRATE 2.7g; FIBER 0.1g; CHOLESTEROL 108mg; IRON 0.9mg; SODIUM 508mg; CALCIUM 35mg

Eat Up—It's Good for You!
Salmon contains high amounts of polyunsaturated omega-3 fatty acids. It's not only good to eat but also may reduce your risk of heart disease.

Chicken, Shrimp, and Sausage Paella

6 servings

prep: 15 minutes   cook: 4 hours

slow-cooker size: 5 quart

1¾ pounds skinned and boned chicken thighs
1 teaspoon dried rosemary
¼ teaspoon black pepper
2 teaspoons vegetable oil

1 (7-ounce) link smoked turkey sausage, sliced
1 (14½-ounce) can organic diced tomatoes with garlic and onion, drained
1 teaspoon paprika
1 teaspoon prepared minced garlic
1½ cups fat-free, less-sodium chicken broth
1 cup frozen petite green peas

1 cup uncooked converted long-grain rice
½ teaspoon ground turmeric (see tip)

¾ pound cooked, peeled and deveined medium-sized shrimp (1½ pounds in shell)

1 Sprinkle chicken thighs evenly with rosemary and pepper. Heat oil in a large skillet over medium-high heat. Add chicken; cook 3 to 4 minutes on each side or until light golden. Arrange chicken in a 5-quart slow cooker.

2 Add sausage to skillet; cook 2 to 3 minutes or until lightly browned. Transfer sausage to slow cooker; add tomatoes and next 4 ingredients.

3 Cover and cook on LOW setting 3 hours. Stir rice and turmeric into slow cooker. Increase heat to HIGH setting; cover and cook 45 minutes.

4 Stir in shrimp; cook on HIGH setting 15 more minutes or until rice is done.

Per 1⅔-cup serving: CALORIES 463 (30% from fat); FAT 15.6g (sat 4.3g, mono 5.4g, poly 3.9g); PROTEIN 45.1g; CARBOHYDRATE 32.5g; FIBER 2.1g; CHOLESTEROL 190mg; IRON 7.5mg; SODIUM 706mg; CALCIUM 68mg

Tune In to Turmeric
Ground turmeric, a common ingredient in curry powders, adds flavor and color to this one-dish meal. Aside from its flavor, turmeric is also touted as an antioxidant, as well as for its anti-inflammatory properties.

Asian-Glazed Chicken Thighs

5 servings

prep: 6 minutes   cook: 6 hours and 4 minutes

slow-cooker size: 3½ or 4 quart

3   tablespoons pure maple syrup
3   tablespoons hoisin sauce
2   tablespoons olive oil
2   tablespoons low-sodium soy sauce
1½ teaspoons Dijon mustard
1   teaspoon prepared minced garlic
½   teaspoon ground red pepper

2   pounds skinned and boned chicken
      thighs
¼   teaspoon salt

¼   cup water
2   tablespoons cornstarch

1 Whisk together first 7 ingredients in a small bowl.

2 Sprinkle chicken thighs evenly with salt; place in a lightly greased 3½- or 4-quart slow cooker. Pour sauce mixture over chicken.

3 Cover and cook on HIGH setting 1 hour. Reduce heat to LOW setting, and cook 5 hours or until chicken is tender.

4 Remove chicken to a serving platter, using a slotted spoon. Whisk together water and cornstarch in a small bowl; add to sauce in slow cooker. Increase heat to HIGH setting; whisk constantly 4 minutes or until sauce begins to thicken. Spoon sauce evenly over chicken.

Per serving (2 thighs): CALORIES 381 (46% from fat); FAT 19.6g (sat 4.6g, mono 9.2g, poly 3.7g); PROTEIN 33.2g; CARBOHYDRATE 15.9g; FIBER 0.1g; CHOLESTEROL 119mg; IRON 1.8mg; SODIUM 523mg; CALCIUM 23mg

66 *Chicken thighs deliver a lot of flavor, and the sauce adds just the right amount of punch to this Asian-inspired dish. Plan on 2 chicken thighs for each serving.* **99**

Moroccan Stew

5 servings

prep: 13 minutes   cook: 4 hours and 5 minutes

slow-cooker size: 3 to 4 quart

1   tablespoon olive oil
1½ pounds skinned and boned chicken
        thighs
2   tablespoons honey
1½ teaspoons curry powder
½   teaspoon ground cinnamon
2   tablespoons dried parsley
1   (14-ounce) can low-sodium chicken
        broth

1½ cups frozen pearl onions, thawed
        and drained
½   cup sliced dried apricots
⅓   cup sliced whole pitted dates
1   lemon, peeled, sectioned, and
        chopped

2   tablespoons all-purpose flour
2   tablespoons water

1   (10-ounce) package couscous,
        cooked
Chopped fresh cilantro (optional)

1 Heat oil in a large skillet over medium-high heat. Add chicken, and cook 5 minutes or until browned. Drain chicken, if necessary; place in a 3- to 4-quart slow cooker. Stir in honey and next 4 ingredients.

2 Cover and cook on HIGH setting 3 hours. Add onions, apricots, dates, and lemon. Cover and cook on HIGH setting 1 more hour.

3 Whisk together flour and water in a small bowl until smooth. Add to slow cooker.

4 Cover and cook on HIGH setting 5 more minutes or until thickened. Serve over couscous and, if desired, with chopped fresh cilantro.

Per serving: CALORIES 570 (21% from fat); FAT 13.5g (sat 3.3g, mono 6g, poly 2.8g); PROTEIN 34.5g; CARBOHYDRATE 78.1g; FIBER 6.2g; CHOLESTEROL 89mg; IRON 3.3mg; SODIUM 330mg; CALCIUM 69mg

66Your taste buds will love this take on a slow-cooked Moroccan stew that's also known as tagine.99

Creamy Chicken and Rice

6 servings

prep: 10 minutes   cook: 5 hours and 45 minutes

slow-cooker size: 4 to 5 quart

1   (6-ounce) package long-grain and
    wild rice mix
6   chicken legs, skinned (about 1¾
    pounds)
1   tablespoon vegetable oil

2   cups water
1   (10¾-ounce) can 98% fat-free
    condensed cream of chicken soup,
    undiluted
¼   cup dry white wine or fat-free,
    less-sodium chicken broth
¼   teaspoon crushed red pepper

1 Remove seasoning packet from rice package; sprinkle chicken with 1½ teaspoons of the seasoning mix. Set aside remaining mix. Heat oil in a large skillet over medium-high heat; add chicken, and cook 7 minutes or until browned, turning occasionally.

2 Combine rice, remaining seasoning mix, water, and remaining 3 ingredients in a 4- to 5-quart slow cooker; top with browned chicken.

3 Cover and cook on LOW setting 5 hours and 45 minutes or until most of the liquid is absorbed. Serve chicken over rice.

Per serving: CALORIES 244 (24% from fat); FAT 6.5g (sat 1.7g, mono 1.9g, poly 1.7g); PROTEIN 19g; CARBOHYDRATE 26g; FIBER 0.5g; CHOLESTEROL 64mg; IRON 1.7mg; SODIUM 635mg; CALCIUM 29mg

66*Talk about comfort food! This creamy sensation takes me down memory lane. It has the same great flavor as the old-time version but with a lot less calories and fat.***99**

Shredded Chicken 'n' Pepper Sandwiches

6 servings

prep: 11 minutes   cook: 5 hours

slow-cooker size: 3½ or 4 quart

1½ pounds chicken tenders
1 (1-pound) package frozen pepper
   stir-fry mix, thawed and drained

⅓ cup balsamic vinegar
2 tablespoons dark brown sugar
1 tablespoon olive oil
⅛ teaspoon salt

6 bagel squares (see tip)
6 slices provolone cheese

1 Place chicken in a 3½- or 4-quart slow cooker; add pepper stir-fry.

2 Combine balsamic vinegar and next 3 ingredients in a small bowl. Pour over chicken.

3 Cover and cook on HIGH setting 1 hour. Reduce heat to LOW setting, and cook 4 hours. Remove chicken from sauce, and shred into large pieces using 2 forks. Return chicken to pan juices. Spoon chicken and vegetables evenly onto bagel bottoms, using a slotted spoon. Top with cheese and bagel tops. Serve immediately.

Per sandwich: CALORIES 429 (26% from fat); FAT 12.4g (sat 5.6g, mono 4.1g, poly 0.9g); PROTEIN 40.3g; CARBOHYDRATE 40g; FIBER 3.2g; CHOLESTEROL 85mg; IRON 3.4mg; SODIUM 669mg; CALCIUM 300mg

Tasty Options
Feel free to toast the bagel squares if you'd like. And if you can't find 'em, just use sub rolls. Serve up the pan juices on the side for dippin' these sandwiches.

153

Turkey Fajitas

10 servings

prep: 6 minutes   cook: 6 hours   marinate: 20 minutes

slow-cooker size: 3 or 3½ quart

2   pounds turkey tenderloins (about
       3 tenderloins)
2   teaspoons vegetable oil
1   (1¼-ounce) package taco seasoning
       mix

1   (16-ounce) package frozen pepper
       stir-fry mix, thawed and drained

10 (7½") 98% fat-free flour tortillas
Toppings: shredded lettuce, light sour
       cream, sliced olives, diced tomato,
       shredded reduced-fat sharp
       Cheddar cheese

1 Cut turkey into 2½" strips. Place in a resealable plastic freezer bag. Add oil and seasoning mix; seal and shake to coat. Marinate in the refrigerator 20 minutes.

2 Place turkey in a 3- or 3½-quart slow cooker; top with stir-fry mix.

3 Cover and cook on HIGH setting 1 hour. Reduce heat to LOW setting, and cook 5 hours.

4 Warm tortillas according to package directions. Spoon turkey mixture evenly in center of each tortilla, using a slotted spoon. Top with desired toppings.

Note: Nutritional analysis does not include optional toppings.

Give chicken a rest, and shake up your menu this week by adding turkey to the list. Turkey tenderloins cook up juicy and tender in this slow-cooker version of fajitas.

Per fajita: CALORIES 245 (10% from fat); FAT 2.7g (sat 0.1g, mono 0.4g, poly 0.5g); PROTEIN 27.5g; CARBOHYDRATE 27.8g; FIBER 3.3g; CHOLESTEROL 36mg; IRON 3.1mg; SODIUM 636mg; CALCIUM 44mg

Red Sauce and Meatballs

(pictured on page 107)

9 servings

prep: 8 minutes   cook: 4 hours

slow-cooker size: 6 quart

1   (25.6-ounce) package frozen
       meatballs, thawed
1   cup frozen chopped onion
2   (28-ounce) cans crushed tomatoes
2   (14.5-ounce) cans organic diced
       tomatoes with basil and garlic
1   tablespoon Italian seasoning
1   tablespoon balsamic vinegar
2   teaspoons prepared minced garlic
½   teaspoon crushed red pepper

14   ounces uncooked spaghetti
Freshly grated Parmesan cheese
       (optional)

1 Combine first 8 ingredients in a 6-quart slow cooker, stirring well.

2 Cover and cook on LOW setting 4 hours.

3 During the last 30 minutes of slow-cook time, cook pasta according to package directions, omitting salt and oil. Serve sauce over pasta; sprinkle with Parmesan cheese, if desired.

Per serving (¾ cup pasta, ¾ cup sauce, and about 8 meatballs): CALORIES 488 (35% from fat); FAT 18.8g (sat 6.7g, mono 0.2g, poly 0.5g); PROTEIN 21g; CARBOHYDRATE 57.2g; FIBER 8.2g; CHOLESTEROL 33mg; IRON 6.2mg; SODIUM 1144mg; CALCIUM 191mg

66Mama mia, this is good! Homemade spaghetti sauce doesn't have to simmer all day to be full of flavor. This version does just fine in only 4 hours.**99**

Greek Lamb and White Bean Chili

10 servings

prep: 7 minutes   cook: 8 hours

slow-cooker size: 5 or 5½ quart

1	pound lean ground lamb
1	cup chopped red onion
3	(15-ounce) cans cannellini beans, rinsed and drained
2	(14½-ounce) cans diced tomatoes with garlic and olive oil, undrained
1	(12-ounce) jar roasted red bell peppers, drained and chopped
1	(14-ounce) can low-sodium beef broth
⅓	cup dry white wine or low-sodium beef broth
¼	cup chopped fresh parsley
1	tablespoon chili powder
2	teaspoons salt-free Greek seasoning
1	cup crumbled reduced-fat feta cheese

Plain yogurt (optional)

Pita bread rounds, cut into wedges (optional)

1 Cook lamb and onion in a large non-stick skillet over medium-high heat, stirring until the lamb crumbles and is no longer pink; drain. Place lamb mixture in a 5- or 5½-quart slow cooker.

2 Process 1 can of beans in a food processor until smooth; add to slow cooker. Stir in remaining beans, tomatoes, and next 6 ingredients.

3 Cover and cook on LOW setting 8 hours. Top with feta cheese. If desired, serve with yogurt and pita rounds.

Per 1-cup serving: CALORIES 238 (38% from fat); FAT 10g (sat 3.5g, mono 2.6g, poly 0.8g); PROTEIN 14.5g; CARBOHYDRATE 20.4g; FIBER 4.1g; CHOLESTEROL 34mg; IRON 2.4mg; SODIUM 810mg; CALCIUM 111mg

66 In this Mediterranean twist on traditional chili, lamb and cannellini beans replace ground beef and kidney beans; then Cheddar cheese and sour cream give way to feta and yogurt. I give this version 2 thumbs up!**99**

156

Pork Roast with Three-Mushroom Ragoût

4 servings

prep: 4 minutes   cook: 8 hours

slow-cooker size: 5 to 6 quart

1   (14.5-ounce) can diced tomatoes
    with Italian herbs, divided
¼   cup all-purpose flour
2   (12-ounce) packages sliced fresh
    button mushrooms
1   (8-ounce) package sliced fresh
    cremini mushrooms (see tip)
1   (1-ounce) package dried porcini
    mushrooms
1   large onion, sliced vertically
6   sun-dried tomatoes, quartered

1¾ pounds boneless pork loin roast
¼   teaspoon salt
¼   teaspoon ground pepper

1 Whisk together ½ can of tomatoes and the flour in a 5- to 6-quart slow cooker. Add mushrooms, onion, and sun-dried tomatoes.

2 Trim fat from pork. Sprinkle pork with salt and pepper; place on top of mushroom mixture. Pour remaining ½ can of tomatoes over pork.

3 Cover and cook on HIGH setting 1 hour. Reduce heat to LOW setting, and cook 7 hours. Remove pork from slow cooker; cut into large chunks. Serve with ragoût over your choice of noodles.

Per serving: CALORIES 527 (35% from fat); FAT 20.3g (sat 7.3g, mono 8.8g, poly 1.9g); PROTEIN 53.8g; CARBOHYDRATE 32.9g; FIBER 6g; CHOLESTEROL 122mg; IRON 4.4mg; SODIUM 662mg; CALCIUM 79mg

Cook's Tips

A ragoût is a French stew with meat, poultry, or fish that's made with or without vegetables.

In this version, you can use 3 packages of button mushrooms if cremini are not available. The slow cooker will be very full before cooking, but the mushrooms will shrink significantly during cooking.

Spicy Sausage, Hominy, and Rice

6 servings

prep: 5 minutes   cook: 6 hours

slow-cooker size: 4 quart

2   cups water
1   (10-ounce) can diced tomatoes with
     lime and cilantro, undrained
1   (15.5-ounce) can white hominy,
     drained
1   (10-ounce) package frozen
     seasoning blend
1   (4.5-ounce) can chopped green
     chilies
1   (12-ounce) package chicken
     sausages with habañero chilies and
     tequila, sliced

½ cup uncooked converted long-grain
     rice

1 Combine first 6 ingredients in a
4-quart slow cooker.

2 Cover and cook on HIGH setting
1 hour. Reduce heat to LOW setting,
and cook 4 hours.

3 Increase heat to HIGH setting; add
rice, and cook 1 hour or until rice is
tender.

Per 1½-cup serving: CALORIES 245 (25% from fat); FAT 6.9g (sat 1.9g, mono 0.1g, poly 0.3g); PROTEIN 11.2g; CARBOHYDRATE 34.7g; FIBER 4.6g; CHOLESTEROL 50mg; IRON 2.1mg; SODIUM 648mg; CALCIUM 31mg

66It's amazing how many flavors you can find at the supermarket these days for canned tomatoes, tomato sauce, and now sausage! Look for this particular sausage or other favorites at your local supermarket.99

Sensational Sides

....

66 *Who says only main dishes are cooked in the slow cooker? I've got some great sides that complement any entrée—so free up your oven or cooktop, and plug in to these sensational sides.* 99

Mr. Food
"OOH IT'S SO GOOD!!"

Green Tomato Sweet Relish

12 to 14 servings

prep: 12 minutes   cook: 11 hours

slow-cooker size: 3 or 3½ quart

2   large green tomatoes, seeded and
     chopped
1   green bell pepper, chopped
½   red bell pepper, chopped
1   cup finely chopped sweet onion
½   cup sugar
2   tablespoons cider vinegar
½   teaspoon ground turmeric
Pinch of cinnamon
¼   teaspoon seafood seasoning

1 Combine all ingredients in a 3- or
3½-quart slow cooker.

2 Cover and cook on LOW setting
11 hours or until vegetables are tender; cool. Store in an airtight container
in the refrigerator up to 1 week.

Your Serve
Serve this relish warm over pork, or try it cold
on top of cream cheese with crackers.

Ratatouille

8 servings

prep: 20 minutes   cook: 8 hours

slow-cooker size: 6 quart

1   large eggplant, cut into 1" cubes
       (about 1½ pounds)
1   (10-ounce) package frozen
       seasoning blend, thawed
1   (14.5-ounce) can diced tomatoes
       with balsamic vinegar, garlic, and
       olive oil, undrained
3   medium zucchini, coarsely chopped
1   tablespoon olive oil
1   tablespoon drained capers
¾   teaspoon salt
½   teaspoon pepper

¼   cup tomato paste
1   (2.25-ounce) can sliced black olives,
       drained
Freshly grated Parmesan cheese

1 Combine first 8 ingredients in a 6-quart slow cooker.

2 Cover and cook on LOW setting 8 hours. Stir in tomato paste and olives. Sprinkle each serving with Parmesan cheese.

Très Versatile

This versatile dish hails from Provence, France. Serve it hot, cold, or at room temperature with roasted lamb; toss it with spaghetti; or offer it as an appetizer over crackers or crostini.

161

German Potato Salad

14 servings

prep: 15 minutes   cook: 6½ hours

slow-cooker size: 6 to 7 quart

3   medium onions, thinly sliced
3   (20-ounce) packages refrigerated
        potato wedges

⅓   cup all-purpose flour
⅓   cup sugar
1   tablespoon dry mustard
2   teaspoons salt
1½ teaspoons celery seeds
1   teaspoon pepper
2   cups water
1¼ cups cider vinegar

3   slices bacon, cooked and crumbled

1 Place onions in a 6- to 7-quart slow cooker. Place potatoes on top of onions.

2 Stir together flour and next 5 ingredients in a large saucepan. Gradually whisk water and vinegar into flour mixture, stirring well with whisk. Cook, whisking constantly, over medium-high heat until slightly thickened; pour over vegetables.

3 Cover and cook on LOW setting 6½ hours. Sprinkle with bacon, and serve warm.

It's so convenient to make German Potato Salad in the slow cooker. Just set your cooker to slow simmer everything well ahead of when company is due. Then, if you'd like, make some hard-cooked eggs and serve 'em sliced over this classic warm potato salad.

Homestyle Baked Beans

10 to 12 servings

prep: 12 minutes   cook: 4 hours

slow-cooker size: 3 to 4 quart

4   slices bacon

1   cup frozen chopped onion
4   (15-ounce) cans pork and beans in
       tomato sauce, drained
¼   cup packed brown sugar
½   cup ketchup
½   cup molasses
1½ teaspoons Worcestershire sauce
1   teaspoon dry mustard
¼   teaspoon ground red pepper

1 Cook bacon in a large skillet over medium heat until done; drain, reserving 1 teaspoon drippings. Crumble bacon.

2 Place bacon, reserved drippings, onion, and remaining ingredients in a 3- to 4-quart slow cooker.

3 Cover and cook on LOW setting 4 hours.

❝*Satisfy the gang at your next gathering with the homestyle goodness of these baked beans. They feed lots of folks, can be served straight from the cooker, and stay warm as long as needed— making this dish the perfect potluck pleaser.*❞

Old-Fashioned Cornbread Dressing

12 to 16 servings

prep: 15 minutes   cook: 4 hours

slow-cooker size: 5½ or 6 quart

4½ cups cornbread crumbs
1 (16-ounce) package herb stuffing
     mix
2 (10¾-ounce) cans cream of chicken
     soup, undiluted
2 (14-ounce) cans low-sodium chicken
     broth
1 medium onion, chopped
½ cup chopped celery
4 large eggs
1 tablespoon rubbed sage
½ teaspoon salt
½ teaspoon pepper

2 tablespoons butter, cut up

1 Stir together first 10 ingredients in a large bowl.

2 Pour cornbread mixture into a lightly greased 5½- or 6-quart slow cooker. Dot with butter.

3 Cover and cook on LOW setting 4 hours or until cooked through and set.

❝Plug in your slow cooker, and cook up this savory dressing for your hungry crowd. It leaves your oven available for more favorites, such as that holiday turkey or pie!❞

Mediterranean Lentils and Rice

6 to 8 servings

prep: 10 minutes   cook: 4 hours and 45 minutes   soak: 8 hours

slow-cooker size: 4 quart

1   cup dried lentils

1   teaspoon salt
1   tablespoon chopped fresh or dried
      rosemary
1   medium onion, chopped
1   cup converted long-grain rice
2   (14-ounce) cans seasoned chicken
      broth with roasted garlic

1   (14.5-ounce) can diced tomatoes,
      undrained
¼   cup chopped kalamata olives
1   (4-ounce) package crumbled feta
      cheese

1 Place lentils in a 4-quart slow cooker. Cover with water 2" above lentils; let soak 8 hours. Drain and rinse; return lentils to slow cooker.

2 Sprinkle lentils with salt and rosemary. Layer onion over lentils; then add rice. Pour broth over layers.

3 Cover and cook on LOW setting 4 hours. Uncover and stir in tomatoes. Cover and cook on LOW setting 45 more minutes or until lentils are tender and liquid is almost absorbed. Gently stir in olives and cheese. Serve immediately.

66*Savor the flavors of the Mediterranean in every bite of this hearty side dish. Increase the serving size, and this protein-packed dish becomes a meatless entrée.*99

Slow-Cooker "Fried" Rice

8 servings

prep: 10 minutes   cook: 2 hours and 45 minutes

slow-cooker size: 4 quart

1   tablespoon dark sesame oil
2   tablespoons olive oil
1¾ cups uncooked converted long-grain
        rice
2   cloves garlic, minced

2   (14.5-ounce) cans chicken broth
1   (1.3-ounce) package hot-and-sour
        soup mix
1   (8-ounce) can sliced water chestnuts,
        drained
1   (16-ounce) package frozen baby
        corn and vegetable blend with
        green peas

2   large eggs, lightly beaten
6   scallions, chopped
Soy sauce

1 Heat oils in a large nonstick skillet over medium-high heat. Add rice and garlic; sauté 4 minutes or until golden.

2 Combine rice mixture, broth, and next 3 ingredients in a 4-quart slow cooker.

3 Cover and cook on HIGH setting 2 hours or until liquid is absorbed and rice is tender.

4 Pour eggs over rice mixture. Cover and cook on HIGH setting 45 more minutes or until egg is set. Stir in scallions, and serve with soy sauce.

66 *You read it correctly! These eggs cook in the slow cooker—no skillet required. But we did bring out the skillet to brown the rice before adding it to the slow cooker. This helps to keep the rice from becoming gummy during the long cooking time. Splurge on dark sesame oil to bring authentic Asian flavor to your "fried" rice.* 99

Black-eyed Peas with a Kick

8 servings

prep: 6 minutes   cook: 4 hours   soak: 8 hours

slow-cooker size: 5 quart

1	(16-ounce) package dried black-eyed peas
¼	cup butter
2	cups hot water
1	(10-ounce) bag frozen seasoning blend, thawed
1	teaspoon prepared minced garlic
1	teaspoon salt
¾	teaspoon crushed red pepper
¼	teaspoon black pepper

1 Sort and wash peas; place in a 5-quart slow cooker. Cover with water 2" above peas; let soak 8 hours. Drain and return peas to slow cooker.

2 Combine butter and remaining ingredients in slow cooker.

3 Cover and cook on HIGH setting 4 hours or until desired degree of doneness.

Ideal Match

Dried peas—and beans—are perfect for slow cooking. Because they're cooked over a long time, they really soak up flavors from the other ingredients.

Braised Red Cabbage

10 to 12 servings

prep: 14 minutes   cook: 3½ hours

slow-cooker size: 5 to 6 quart

1	medium-sized red cabbage, shredded (about 2¾ pounds)
2	Granny Smith apples, peeled and sliced
¼	cup butter
¼	cup dry red wine (see tip)
1	bay leaf
3	tablespoons brown sugar
1	teaspoon salt
¼	teaspoon pepper
¼	teaspoon ground cloves

1 Combine all ingredients in a 5- to 6-quart slow cooker.

2 Cover and cook on LOW setting 3½ hours or until liquid is absorbed and cabbage is tender. **Remove and discard bay leaf.**

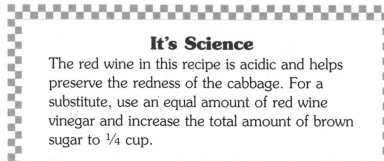

It's Science

The red wine in this recipe is acidic and helps preserve the redness of the cabbage. For a substitute, use an equal amount of red wine vinegar and increase the total amount of brown sugar to ¼ cup.

Orange-Kissed Carrots

6 servings

prep: 5 minutes   cook: 6 hours

slow-cooker size: 3 to 4 quart

2 tablespoons butter, melted
2 pounds baby carrots
½ teaspoon ground ginger
¼ teaspoon salt
½ teaspoon pepper
¼ cup orange marmalade

1 Stir together all ingredients in a 3- to 4-quart slow cooker, coating carrots well.

2 Cover and cook on HIGH setting 5½ to 6 hours or until carrots are tender.

66My secret to these sumptuous carrots? Orange marmalade! The glaze mixture lightly 'kisses' these carrots, making them a hands-down favorite for all ages.99

Down-Home Collard Greens

6 servings

prep: 13 minutes   cook: 9 hours

slow-cooker size: 6-quart oval

1   meaty smoked ham hock, rinsed
1   large carrot, chopped
1½ cups frozen chopped onion

1   (1-pound) package chopped fresh
        collard greens, tough stems
        removed
1   teaspoon prepared roasted minced
        garlic
½   teaspoon crushed red pepper
¼   teaspoon black pepper

3   (14-ounce) cans seasoned chicken
        broth with roasted garlic
2¾ cups water

1 Place first 3 ingredients in a 6-quart oval slow cooker.

2 Add collard greens. Sprinkle greens with garlic, crushed red pepper, and black pepper.

3 Pour broth and water over greens, pressing greens down into liquid as much as possible with a large spoon.

4 Cover and cook on LOW setting 9 hours. Remove greens to a serving dish with a slotted spoon or tongs. Remove meat from ham hock, discarding fat and bones. Chop meat; add to greens, tossing lightly to evenly distribute meat in greens. Ladle desired amount of pot liquor over greens.

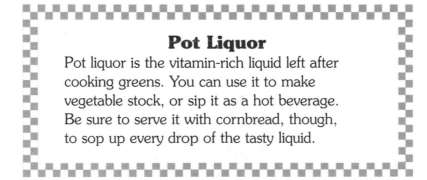

Pot Liquor
Pot liquor is the vitamin-rich liquid left after cooking greens. You can use it to make vegetable stock, or sip it as a hot beverage. Be sure to serve it with cornbread, though, to sop up every drop of the tasty liquid.

Cheesy Mexican Corn Pudding

8 servings

prep: 10 minutes   cook: 5 hours

slow-cooker size: 3-quart oval

2   large eggs
1   (15.25-ounce) can corn with red
      and green bell peppers, undrained
1   (14¾-ounce) can cream-style corn
1   (4.5-ounce) can diced green chilies
1   (8.5-ounce) box corn muffin mix
½   cup butter, melted
½   cup shredded Monterey Jack cheese

1 Whisk eggs in a large bowl until frothy. Add corn and remaining ingredients; mix well. Pour into a lightly greased 3-quart oval slow cooker.

2 Cover and cook on LOW setting 5 hours or until edges are set. Stir before serving.

" *These ordinary products dress up a box of corn muffin mix to make an extra-ordinary side dish fit for company.* **"**

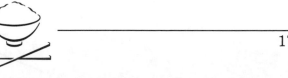

Corn on the Cob with Bacon and Herbed Butter

(pictured on facing page)

12 servings

prep: 12 minutes   cook: 3 hours

slow-cooker size: 5 quart

6   tablespoons butter, softened
4   cloves garlic, pressed
½   teaspoon dried dillweed
1   teaspoon freshly ground black
        pepper
½   teaspoon salt
6   ears fresh corn, husks removed

12   fully cooked slices bacon
½   cup chicken broth
1   red bell pepper, chopped

1 Combine first 5 ingredients in a small bowl. Rub butter mixture evenly over ears of corn. Cut each ear in half.

2 Wrap each half with 1 slice of bacon, and secure with wooden toothpicks. Place corn in a single layer in a 5-quart slow cooker (see tip). Add broth and bell pepper.

3 Cover and cook on LOW setting 3 hours or until corn is tender. Remove bacon before serving, if desired.

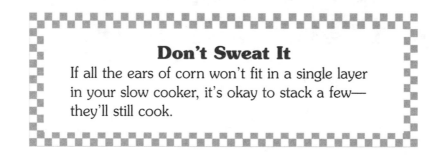

Don't Sweat It
If all the ears of corn won't fit in a single layer in your slow cooker, it's okay to stack a few—they'll still cook.

Brownie–Cream Cheese
Pudding Cake, page 202

Chocolate- and Peppermint-Coated Pretzels,
page 189

Cheddar, Potato, and Bacon Gratin

(pictured on facing page)

8 to 10 servings

prep: 9 minutes   cook: 2½ hours

slow-cooker size: 3½ or 4 quart

2   (10¾-ounce) cans Cheddar cheese
        soup, undiluted
¼   teaspoon garlic powder
1   teaspoon freshly ground pepper

2   (20-ounce) packages refrigerated
        sliced potatoes
12   fully cooked slices bacon, crumbled
1   cup (4 ounces) shredded sharp
        Cheddar cheese
3   tablespoons butter

1 Combine soup, garlic powder, and
pepper in a small bowl.

2 Layer half the potatoes in a lightly
greased 3½- or 4-quart slow cooker;
sprinkle with half the bacon, and pour
half the soup mixture evenly over potatoes. Repeat layers, ending with soup
mixture; sprinkle shredded cheese over
top, and dot with butter.

3 Cover and cook on HIGH setting
2½ hours or until potatoes are fork-
tender. Let stand 10 minutes.

*66Refrigerated sliced potatoes are the key to
making this no-fuss side dish a winner with
your gang. And by using precooked bacon,
it's truly hands-off cooking—my kinda recipe!99*

Rustic Homestyle Potatoes

8 servings

prep: 5 minutes   cook: 5 hours

slow-cooker size: 5 quart

1   (30-ounce) package frozen country-
        style hashbrowns
1   (10¾-ounce) can cream of potato
        soup, undiluted (see tip)
1⅓ cups milk
1   tablespoon butter
½   teaspoon salt
¾   teaspoon pepper

1   cup (4 ounces) shredded sharp
        Cheddar cheese

1 Combine first 6 ingredients in a
lightly greased 5-quart slow cooker.

2 Cover and cook on LOW setting
5 hours. Stir in cheese, and serve
immediately.

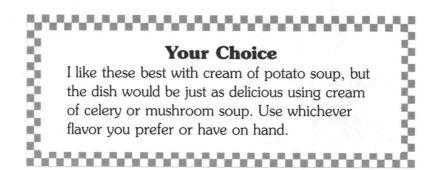

Your Choice
I like these best with cream of potato soup, but
the dish would be just as delicious using cream
of celery or mushroom soup. Use whichever
flavor you prefer or have on hand.

Green Bean Casserole

8 to 10 servings

prep: 6 minutes   cook: 2½ hours

slow-cooker size: 2 to 3 quart

2   (14.5-ounce) cans cut green beans,
      drained
1   (10¾-ounce) can cream of
      mushroom soup, undiluted
1   (8-ounce) package shredded
      Cheddar cheese
2   (4.5-ounce) jars sliced mushrooms,
      drained
1   cup milk
1   tablespoon Worcestershire sauce
¼   teaspoon pepper
1   (6-ounce) can French fried onion
      rings, divided

1 Combine first 7 ingredients in a large bowl; stir in half the French fried onion rings. Spoon casserole mixture into a lightly greased 2- to 3-quart slow cooker.

2 Cover and cook on LOW setting 2 hours.

3 Sprinkle remaining onion rings on top of casserole. Cover and cook on LOW setting 30 more minutes.

❝ *"If your holiday menu has your oven bursting from too many casseroles baking in it, bring out your slow cooker and cook up this family favorite. It's just as tasty made this way as it is made using the traditional method. Take it from me when I say, 'Ooh it's SLOW good!'* ❞

Zesty Creamed Spinach

8 to 10 servings

prep: 11 minutes   cook: 2 hours

slow-cooker size: 3 or 3½ quart

4   (10-ounce) packages frozen
     chopped spinach, thawed,
     drained, and squeezed dry
2   (8-ounce) containers chive-and-
     onion cream cheese
1   (8-ounce) package pasteurized
     prepared cheese product, cubed
⅓   cup butter, melted
2   tablespoons all-purpose flour
1   tablespoon Worcestershire sauce
¼   teaspoon black pepper
¼   teaspoon ground red pepper

1 Stir together all ingredients in a large
  bowl. Spoon into a lightly greased
3- or 3½-quart slow cooker.

2 Cover and cook on LOW setting
  2 hours. Stir well before serving.

66*Eating your spinach is no problem when
it's combined with 2 types of cheese and a zip
of red pepper. Thanks, Mom!*99

"Squashed" Dressing

8 servings

prep: 18 minutes   cook: 3 hours

slow-cooker size: 5 quart

2   pounds yellow squash, sliced
½   cup chopped green bell pepper
½   cup chopped onion
¼   cup butter

5   cups crumbled cornbread
1   (10¾-ounce) can cream of chicken
       soup, undiluted
1½ cups milk
½   teaspoon salt
½   teaspoon black pepper

1 Combine first 4 ingredients in a large microwave-safe bowl. Cover with plastic wrap, and microwave at HIGH 8 minutes; drain.

2 Combine squash mixture, cornbread crumbs, and remaining ingredients in a lightly greased 5-quart slow cooker.

3 Cover and cook on HIGH setting 3 hours or until lightly browned. Let stand 15 minutes before serving.

66Serve this dish as a new alternative to your holiday side dishes—it's a tasty cross between a squash casserole and cornbread dressing. And as an added plus, it frees up valuable oven space!99

Simple Mashed Sweet Potatoes

6 servings

prep: 11 minutes   cook: 5½ hours

slow-cooker size: 4 to 5 quart

4 sweet potatoes, peeled and
  shredded (about 2 pounds)
  (see tip)
⅓ cup orange juice
¼ cup butter
¼ cup packed brown sugar
½ teaspoon salt

½ cup chopped pecans, toasted

1 Combine first 5 ingredients in a lightly greased 4- to 5-quart slow cooker.

2 Cover and cook on LOW setting 5½ hours or until potatoes are tender. Using a potato masher, mash potatoes in cooker to desired consistency. Sprinkle with toasted pecans before serving.

It's a Snap!
Shred the sweet potatoes in a snap in a food processor. This helps the potatoes cook evenly and creates a smoother mash. The potatoes shrink down in the slow cooker as they soften, so there's plenty of room to mash right in the cooker when the potatoes are tender.

Slow &
Sweet

....

66Mmm … good! That
sums up this chapter of
sweet treats. Indulge your
gang with some of the best
desserts ever—all from
your slow cooker! Ooh,
they're SLOW good!**99**

Mexican Hot Mocha

8 servings

prep: 2 minutes   cook: 3 hours

slow-cooker size: 4 quart

8   cups milk
1   cup (6 ounces) mini semisweet
       chocolate chips (see tip)
½   cup confectioners' sugar
¼   cup instant coffee granules
½   teaspoon ground cinnamon
¼   teaspoon ground nutmeg

Sweetened whipped cream (optional)
Grated semisweet chocolate (optional)

1 Combine first 6 ingredients in a 4-quart slow cooker.

2 Cover and cook on LOW setting 3 hours or until thoroughly heated and chocolate is melted, whisking after 2 hours. Whisk again before serving. Serve with whipped cream and grated chocolate, if desired.

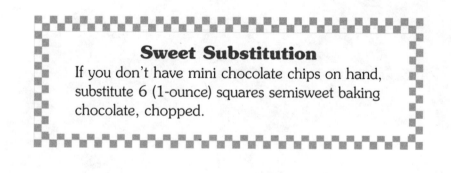

Sweet Substitution
If you don't have mini chocolate chips on hand, substitute 6 (1-ounce) squares semisweet baking chocolate, chopped.

Spirited Apple Butter

4 cups

prep: 13 minutes   cook: 10 hours   chill: 8 hours

slow-cooker size: 3 or 3½ quarts

3	pounds Granny Smith apples, peeled and sliced
¼	cup lemon juice
2	tablespoons brandy (see tip)
1½	cups granulated sugar
½	cup packed light brown sugar
½	teaspoon ground nutmeg
½	teaspoon ground cinnamon

1 Combine all ingredients in a 3- or 3½-quart slow cooker.

2 Cover and cook on LOW setting 10 hours. Mash apple mixture; cool. Cover and chill 8 hours or overnight.

Butter Bits

This apple butter can be stored in the refrigerator up to 1 week. It's perfect for slathering over toast or biscuits.

If you'd prefer not to use brandy, then substitute 2 tablespoons apple cider.

Tart Triple-Berry Sauce

8 to 10 servings

prep: 9 minutes   cook: 5 hours

slow-cooker size: 4 quart

1¼ cups packed brown sugar
¼   cup all-purpose flour
1   (16-ounce) package frozen
        blackberries
1   (16-ounce) package frozen
        strawberries
1   (16-ounce) package frozen
        raspberries
2   tablespoons lemon zest, minced
1   tablespoon lemon juice

1   tablespoon butter, softened
2   teaspoons vanilla extract

1 Stir together brown sugar and flour in a 4-quart slow cooker. Add berries, lemon zest, and lemon juice, tossing to coat.

2 Cover and cook on LOW setting 5 hours. Stir in butter and vanilla. Serve immediately, or chill until cooled. Store in the refrigerator. Serve over ice cream, pound cake, waffles, or other dessert.

Triple the Benefits

This tart sauce—rich in antioxidants, thanks to the berries—is perfect served over ice cream or angel food cake, if you're watching your waistline. Try bottling the sauce around the holidays for a yummy festive gift; it makes a little over 6 cups.

Saucy Apples 'n' Pears

10 servings

prep: 9 minutes   cook: 5 hours and 15 minutes

slow-cooker size: 5 quart

3   cooking apples, peeled (about
       1½ pounds)
3   ripe pears, peeled (about 1½
       pounds)
¼   cup raisins

½   cup pure maple syrup
¼   cup butter, melted
½   cup packed dark brown sugar
1   tablespoon lemon juice
2   (3") sticks cinnamon

2   tablespoons cornstarch
2   tablespoons water

½   cup chopped pecans

1 Core and slice apples and pears; place in a 5-quart slow cooker. Sprinkle with raisins.

2 Combine syrup and next 3 ingredients, stirring well. Pour butter mixture over fruit; toss to coat. Tuck cinnamon sticks into mixture.

3 Cover and cook on LOW setting 5 hours. Increase heat to HIGH setting. Combine cornstarch and water, stirring until smooth; gently stir mixture into fruit.

4 Cover and cook on HIGH setting 15 more minutes or until thickened; remove cinnamon sticks. Serve warm over ice cream or waffles; sprinkle each serving with pecans.

Note: Store leftovers, covered, in the refrigerator. Reheat in the microwave until warm; avoid stirring as much as possible so as not to break up fruit. You can also serve this as a side dish with pork chops or pork tenderloin.

❝*When entertaining the gang, serve this fruity dish directly from the slow cooker so that it stays nice and warm.*❞

187

S'mores Fondue

24 servings

prep: 10 minutes   cook: 1½ hours

slow-cooker size: 3 quart

1   (14-ounce) can sweetened
      condensed milk
2   teaspoons ground allspice
½   cup fat-free caramel topping
1   (16-ounce) package chocolate-
      flavored bark candy coating,
      broken into chunks
¼   cup dark chocolate chips

Graham cracker sticks
Marshmallows

1 Combine first 3 ingredients in a
3-quart slow cooker; add chocolate-
flavored bark candy coating and chocolate chips.

2 Cover and cook on LOW setting
1½ hours. Stir and serve fondue
with graham cracker sticks and
marshmallows.

Tasty Tip
To make more traditional s'mores, "toast"
marshmallows by broiling them 1 to 2 minutes
or until light golden. Place 1 marshmallow on a
graham cracker sheet, and spoon fondue over
it. Place another graham cracker sheet over the
marshmallow to form a sandwich.

Chocolate- and Peppermint-Coated Pretzels

(pictured on page 175)

80 pieces (about 4½ pounds)

prep: 15 minutes   cook: 2 hours

slow-cooker size: 6 quart

1   (16-ounce) package pretzel nuggets
2   (16-ounce) packages chocolate-
    flavored bark candy coating,
    coarsely chopped
2   cups (12 ounces) semisweet
    chocolate chips
1   (4-ounce) square semisweet baking
    chocolate, broken into pieces

1   (16-ounce) package hard
    peppermint candies, finely crushed
    and divided (about 1½ cups)
½   teaspoon peppermint extract

1 Combine first 4 ingredients in a 6-quart slow cooker.

2 Cover and cook on LOW setting 2 hours. Stir chocolate mixture; add 1 cup crushed peppermint candies and peppermint extract, stirring well to coat.

3 Drop pretzel mixture by heaping tablespoonfuls onto wax paper. Sprinkle remaining ½ cup crushed peppermint candies evenly on pieces before they set. Let stand until firm. Store in an airtight container. (See tip on page 190.)

The slow cooker is ideal for candy making. It keeps chocolate at a constant temperature, so no reheating is necessary to get an even coating.

Cherry-Vanilla-Macadamia Nut Clusters

about 32 pieces (3 pounds)

prep: 10 minutes   cook: 1½ hours

slow-cooker size: 3 to 4 quart

16 (2-ounce) vanilla-flavored almond
   bark candy coating squares, cut
   in half
2 cups macadamia nuts, toasted and
   coarsely chopped

1 (3-ounce) can chow mein noodles
1 cup dried cherries

1 Combine chocolate and nuts in a
  3- to 4-quart slow cooker.

2 Cover and cook on LOW setting
  1½ hours or until melted. Stir chocolate mixture. Add chow mein noodles and dried cherries, stirring well to coat.

3 Drop mixture by heaping table-
  spoonfuls onto wax paper. Let stand until firm (see tip). Store in an airtight container.

Cool It!
If you can't wait for the candies to harden at room temperature, try popping them in the fridge for a quick cooldown.

Crispy Chocolate Chip Treats

3 dozen

prep: 35 minutes   cook: 1 hour

slow-cooker size: 3 to 4 quart

¼   cup butter
2   tablespoons light brown sugar
½   teaspoon vanilla extract
1   (10-ounce) bag marshmallows

6   cups crisp rice cereal
½   cup semisweet chocolate chips

1 Combine first 4 ingredients in a 3- to 4-quart slow cooker.

2 Cover and cook on LOW setting 1 hour. Stir marshmallow mixture (see tip). Add cereal and chocolate chips, stirring well to coat.

3 Drop cereal mixture by heaping tablespoonfuls onto wax paper. Let stand until firm. (See tip on opposite page.) Store in an airtight container.

Shapely Treats

You can also press cereal mixture into a 9" x 13" pan and cut into desired pieces; or scoop out mixture with a cookie scoop. Use cooking spray on spoons, scoops, and hands to help minimize the stickiness.

Crunchy Peanut Butter and Chocolate Candies

60 pieces (5 pounds)

prep: 5 minutes   cook: 2 hours

slow-cooker size: 3½ or 4 quart

1   (16-ounce) jar dry-roasted peanuts
1   (10-ounce) package swirled
        chocolate and peanut butter chips
18   (2-ounce) chocolate-flavored bark
        candy coating squares, cut in half

1   (14-ounce) package corn-and-rice
        cereal

½   cup confectioners' sugar (optional)

1 Combine first 3 ingredients in a 3½- or 4-quart slow cooker.

2 Cover and cook on LOW setting 2 hours or until melted. Stir chocolate mixture. Add cereal, stirring well to coat.

3 Drop cereal mixture by heaping tablespoonfuls onto wax paper. Let stand until firm. (See tip on page 190.) Sift confectioners' sugar over the candies, if desired. Store in an airtight container.

66You gotta love the popular combination of chocolate and peanut butter—and these candies are no exception! 99

Berries 'n' Cream Oatmeal

8 servings

prep: 10 minutes   cook: 3 hours

slow-cooker size: 3½ quart

3 cups uncooked regular oats
2 (5-ounce) packages dried berry blend
½ cup packed light brown sugar
1 tablespoon vanilla extract
½ teaspoon salt
4 cups milk
3 cups water
2 tablespoons butter

1 cup sliced almonds, toasted

1 Combine first 8 ingredients in a 3½-quart slow cooker.

2 Cover and cook on LOW setting 3 hours or until thickened. Stir in almonds. Serve warm.

Berry Good!

Jump-start your morning with this creamy treat. Go ahead and cook the oatmeal ahead of time, and then all you have to do is reheat it in the microwave when you're ready to eat it. Stir well before serving. It keeps in the fridge up to 1 week.

Apple-Crunch Cobbler

8 servings

prep: 11 minutes   cook: 6 hours

slow-cooker size: 4 quart

4   medium Granny Smith apples,
        peeled and sliced
3   cups granola cereal, divided
½   cup golden raisins
¼   cup honey
¼   cup packed brown sugar
2   tablespoons butter, melted
1   teaspoon vanilla extract
1   teaspoon ground cinnamon
¼   teaspoon ground nutmeg
⅛   teaspoon ground cloves

1   cup chopped walnuts, toasted
¼   cup packed brown sugar
8   cups vanilla ice cream

1 Place apples in a lightly greased 4-quart slow cooker. Combine 2 cups granola cereal and next 8 ingredients in a medium bowl; sprinkle over apples. Cover and cook on LOW setting 6 hours.

2 Combine remaining 1 cup granola cereal, the walnuts, and ¼ cup brown sugar. Serve apples over vanilla ice cream, and sprinkle with granola topping.

"I love how this comforting mix of spiced apples and crunchy granola comes together over yummy vanilla ice cream.**"**

Blueberries 'n' Dumplings

(pictured on page 4)

6 servings

prep: 15 minutes   cook: 3 hours

slow-cooker size: 5-quart round

1¼ cups sugar
3 tablespoons all-purpose flour
2 teaspoons grated lemon rind

2 (16-ounce) packages frozen
   blueberries

1½ cups biscuit mix
2 tablespoons sugar
3 tablespoons butter
1 (8-ounce) container sour cream

Slow-Cookin' Tips

• Remove slow-cooker lid carefully to prevent condensation from dripping onto dumplings and making them soggy.

• Some slow cookers have hot spots. To ensure that the dumplings become an even golden color, rotate the insert a half turn about halfway through cooking—but don't remove the lid.

1 Stir together first 3 ingredients in a 3-quart saucepan until blended.

2 Stir in blueberries. Cook, stirring constantly, over medium heat until sugar dissolves. Increase heat to medium-high, and bring mixture to a boil, stirring often. Cook about 5 minutes or until thickened, stirring often.

3 Meanwhile, combine biscuit mix and 2 tablespoons sugar in a medium bowl. Cut in butter with a pastry blender or 2 forks until crumbly; add sour cream, stirring until dry ingredients are moistened and a soft dough forms.

4 Pour hot blueberry filling into a 5-quart round slow cooker. Carefully drop dough in 6 large spoonfuls on top of filling.

5 Cover and cook on LOW setting 3 hours or until dumplings are golden (see tips).

Glazed Pears with Hazelnuts

6 servings

prep: 15 minutes   cook: 4 hours

slow-cooker size: 5 quart

½   cup butter, softened
⅓   cup packed light brown sugar
2   tablespoons chopped hazelnuts, toasted
2   tablespoons golden raisins
⅛   teaspoon ground nutmeg
⅛   teaspoon ground cinnamon
6   Bosc pears, peeled, cored, and halved (see note)
3   tablespoons ruby port (optional) (see tip)

Vanilla ice cream
Caramel topping

1 Combine first 6 ingredients in a medium bowl, stirring until well combined. Spoon butter mixture evenly into each cored pear half. Place pears in a 5-quart slow cooker. Pour port over pears, if desired.

2 Cover and cook on LOW setting 4 hours or until pears are tender but still hold their shape. Serve warm with ice cream and caramel topping.

Note: Make sure you use firm, ripe pears.

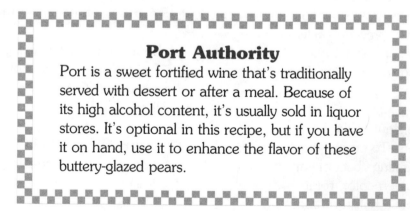

Port Authority

Port is a sweet fortified wine that's traditionally served with dessert or after a meal. Because of its high alcohol content, it's usually sold in liquor stores. It's optional in this recipe, but if you have it on hand, use it to enhance the flavor of these buttery-glazed pears.

Fruity Rice Pudding

10 servings

prep: 13 minutes   cook: 4 hours

slow-cooker size: 3-quart oval

3¾ cups milk
1   cup uncooked Arborio rice (see tip)
1   cup sugar
½   teaspoon ground cinnamon
¼   teaspoon salt
3   tablespoons butter, melted
1   teaspoon vanilla extract
½   cup dried apricots, chopped
½   cup chopped shelled pistachios

1 Combine all ingredients in a 3-quart oval slow cooker, stirring well.

2 Cover and cook on HIGH setting 2½ hours. Stir mixture; cover and cook on HIGH setting 1½ more hours.

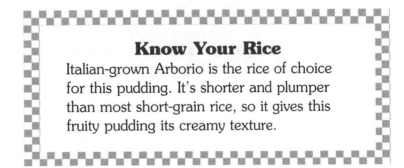

Know Your Rice
Italian-grown Arborio is the rice of choice for this pudding. It's shorter and plumper than most short-grain rice, so it gives this fruity pudding its creamy texture.

Chocolate Candy Bar Bread Pudding

8 servings

prep: 12 minutes   cook: 2 hours

slow-cooker size: 3 to 4 quart

2   cups packed brown sugar
⅓   cup unsweetened cocoa
1   cup milk
½   cup butter, melted
3   large eggs, lightly beaten
2   teaspoons vanilla extract
5   cups torn firm white bread
1   cup chopped chocolate-coated
        caramel and creamy nougat bars
        (see tip)

Caramel topping
Additional chopped chocolate-coated
        caramel and creamy nougat bars

1 Stir together first 6 ingredients in a medium bowl until blended. Stir in bread and candy. Pour into a lightly greased 3- to 4-quart slow cooker.

2 Cover and cook on LOW setting 2 hours or until center is set (but still jiggles). Top each serving with caramel topping and additional chopped candy bars.

Chocolate Delight

Try making this bread pudding with your favorite chocolate candy bar. The popular ones are peanut butter and creamy coconut, but the options are endless!

Spiced Bourbon-Pecan Rice Pudding

6 to 8 servings

prep: 5 minutes   cook: 3 hours

slow-cooker size: 3 or 3½ quart

3   cups cooked long-grain rice (see tip)
½   cup raisins or sweetened dried
        cranberries
1   teaspoon vanilla extract
1   (14-ounce) can sweetened
        condensed milk
1   (12-ounce) can evaporated milk
¼   cup bourbon
2   tablespoons light brown sugar
1   teaspoon pumpkin pie spice

1   cup chopped pecans, toasted

1 Combine first 8 ingredients in a lightly greased 3- or 3½-quart slow cooker.

2 Cover and cook on LOW setting 3 hours or until liquid is mostly absorbed. Stir before serving, and sprinkle with pecans. Serve warm or chilled.

Right Rice
Be sure to use only cooked long-grain white rice in this recipe. Cooked instant rice will break down during the long cooking time, causing a mushy texture.

Chocolate-Coconut Bread Pudding

6 to 8 servings

prep: 11 minutes   cook: 2 hours and 45 minutes   chill: 1 hour

slow-cooker size: 4 to 5 quart

3   large eggs
2   (13.5-ounce) cans coconut milk
¾   cup sugar
1   teaspoon ground cinnamon
¼   teaspoon ground nutmeg
¼   teaspoon salt
1   (12-ounce) day-old French bread
     loaf, cut into 1" cubes
1   cup sweetened flaked coconut
1   cup (6 ounces) semisweet chocolate
     chips

Sweetened whipped cream (optional)

1 Whisk together first 6 ingredients in a large bowl. Add bread cubes, coconut, and chocolate chips, stirring gently just until bread is moistened. Cover and chill 1 hour. Pour mixture into a lightly greased 4- to 5-quart slow cooker.

2 Cover and cook on LOW setting 2 hours and 45 minutes or until set. Serve with sweetened whipped cream, if desired.

"You'll go nuts over this bread pudding, with its combination of chocolate and coconut! Canned coconut milk is available in the ethnic foods section of most supermarkets.**"**

Cinnamon-Raisin Bread Pudding

6 to 8 servings

prep: 10 minutes   cook: 2 hours   stand: 30 minutes

slow-cooker size: 4-quart round

3   large eggs
½   cup packed light brown sugar
½   teaspoon ground nutmeg
1   cup milk
1   cup whipping cream
1   teaspoon vanilla extract
¼   cup butter, melted
1   (1-pound) cinnamon-raisin bread
       loaf, cut into 1" cubes
½   cup butterscotch chips
½   cup chopped pecans, toasted

Sweetened whipped cream (optional)

1 Whisk together first 3 ingredients in a large bowl; stir in milk and next 3 ingredients. Add bread cubes, stirring until moistened. Stir in butterscotch chips and pecans. Pour into a lightly greased 4-quart round slow cooker.

2 Cover and cook on LOW setting 2 hours or until center is set. Carefully remove slow cooker insert from heat element. Let stand, covered, 30 minutes. Serve pudding warm with whipped cream, if desired.

Crazy for Cinnamon

For more cinnamon flavor, you can substitute an equal amount of cinnamon chips for the butterscotch chips. Cinnamon chips tend to be a seasonal item—available only during the holiday months—so, if you love 'em, stock up.

Brownie–Cream Cheese Pudding Cake

(pictured on page 174)

6 servings

prep: 15 minutes   cook: 5½ hours   stand: 45 minutes

slow-cooker size: 3 quart

1   (18-ounce) package brownie mix
2   large eggs
¼   cup vegetable oil
2   tablespoons water

1   (8-ounce) package cream cheese,
       softened
¼   cup butter, softened
½   cup sugar
2   large eggs
1   teaspoon vanilla extract
2   tablespoons all-purpose flour
½   cup milk chocolate chips

1 Stir together first 4 ingredients in a medium bowl until batter is smooth. Spoon half of brownie batter into a lightly greased 3-quart slow cooker.

2 Beat cream cheese and butter at medium speed of an electric beater until creamy; gradually add sugar, beating well. Add 2 eggs, 1 at a time, beating until blended. Stir in vanilla. Fold in flour and chocolate chips. Pour cream cheese mixture over brownie batter in slow cooker. Dollop remaining brownie batter over cream cheese mixture; swirl mixture gently with a knife.

3 Cover and cook on LOW setting 5½ hours or until set. Carefully remove slow cooker insert from heat element; let stand 45 minutes before serving.

"One bite will have everyone saying, 'OOH IT'S SO GOOD!!'® Be sure to save some of this decadent dessert for yourself because there won't be any left after the gang's been served.**"**

Rocky Road Pudding Cake

6 to 8 servings

prep: 7 minutes   cook: 2½ hours   stand: 30 minutes

slow-cooker size: 3½-quart round

½   cup butter, melted
1⅓ cups sugar
1   cup all-purpose flour
4   large eggs, lightly beaten
⅓   cup unsweetened cocoa
¼   cup chopped pecans
½   teaspoon ground cinnamon
¼   teaspoon salt
2   teaspoons vanilla extract

1   cup miniature marshmallows
Vanilla ice cream (optional)

1 Stir together first 9 ingredients in a large bowl. Pour into a lightly greased 3½-quart round slow cooker.

2 Cover and cook on LOW setting 2½ hours or until set around the edges but still soft in the center. Sprinkle with marshmallows; let stand, covered, 30 minutes. Serve warm with ice cream, if desired.

After cooking 2½ hours, the center of this mixture is still a little jiggly—but don't cook it any longer. Just keep it covered, and let it stand 30 minutes. It'll be a great pudding-cake consistency.

METRIC EQUIVALENTS

The recipes that appear in this cookbook use the standard U.S. method for measuring liquid and dry or solid ingredients (teaspoons, tablespoons, and cups). The information in the following charts is provided to help cooks outside the United States successfully use these recipes. All equivalents are approximate.

EQUIVALENTS FOR DIFFERENT TYPES OF INGREDIENTS

A standard cup measure of a dry or solid ingredient will vary in weight depending on the type of ingredient. A standard cup of liquid is the same volume for any type of liquid. Use the following chart when converting standard cup measures to grams (weight) or milliliters (volume).

Standard Cup	Fine Powder (ex. flour)	Grain (ex. rice)	Granular (ex. sugar)	Liquid Solids (ex. butter)	Liquid (ex. milk)
1	140 g	150 g	190 g	200 g	240 ml
¾	105 g	113 g	143 g	150 g	180 ml
⅔	93 g	100 g	125 g	133 g	160 ml
½	70 g	75 g	95 g	100 g	120 ml
⅓	47 g	50 g	63 g	67 g	80 ml
¼	35 g	38 g	48 g	50 g	60 ml
⅛	18 g	19 g	24 g	25 g	30 ml

DRY INGREDIENTS BY WEIGHT

(To convert ounces to grams, multiply the number of ounces by 30.)

1 oz	=	¹⁄₁₆ lb	=	30 g
4 oz	=	¼ lb	=	120 g
8 oz	=	½ lb	=	240 g
12 oz	=	¾ lb	=	360 g
16 oz	=	1 lb	=	480 g

LENGTH

(To convert inches to centimeters, multiply the number of inches by 2.5.)

1 in			=	2.5 cm		
6 in	=	½ ft	=	15 cm		
12 in	=	1 ft	=	30 cm		
36 in	=	3 ft	= 1 yd	=	90 cm		
40 in			=	100 cm	=	1 meter

LIQUID INGREDIENTS BY VOLUME

¼ tsp						=	1 ml
½ tsp						=	2 ml
1 tsp						=	5 ml
3 tsp	=	1 tbls			= ½ fl oz	=	15 ml
		2 tbls	=	⅛ cup	= 1 fl oz	=	30 ml
		4 tbls	=	¼ cup	= 2 fl oz	=	60 ml
		5⅓ tbls	=	⅓ cup	= 3 fl oz	=	80 ml
		8 tbls	=	½ cup	= 4 fl oz	=	120 ml
		10⅔ tbls	=	⅔ cup	= 5 fl oz	=	160 ml
		12 tbls	=	¾ cup	= 6 fl oz	=	180 ml
		16 tbls	=	1 cup	= 8 fl oz	=	240 ml
		1 pt	=	2 cups	= 16 fl oz	=	480 ml
		1 qt	=	4 cups	= 32 fl oz	=	960 ml
					33 fl oz	=	1000 ml	= 1 liter

COOKING/OVEN TEMPERATURES

	Fahrenheit	Celsius	Gas Mark
Freeze Water	32° F	0° C	
Room Temperature	68° F	20° C	
Boil Water	212° F	100° C	
Bake	325° F	160° C	3
	350° F	180° C	4
	375° F	190° C	5
	400° F	200° C	6
	425° F	220° C	7
	450° F	230° C	8
Broil			Grill

Index

FAVORITE RECIPES

Jot down the family's and your favorite recipes for handy-dandy fast reference.
And don't forget to include the dishes that drew "oohs" and "aahs" when you had the gang over.

Recipe	Source/Page	Remarks